W9-CLX-564

HAUNTED OHIO III:

Still More Ghostly Tales from the Buckeye State

CHRIS WOODYARD

Kestrel
Publications

1811 Stonewood Drive
Beavercreek, OH 45432

ALSO BY CHRIS WOODYARD

Haunted Ohio: Ghostly Tales from the Buckeye State
Haunted Ohio II: More Ghostly Tales from the Buckeye State
Haunted Ohio III: Still More Ghostly Tales from the Buckeye State
Haunted Ohio IV: Restless Spirits
Haunted Ohio V: 200 Years of Ghosts
Spooky Ohio: 13 Traditional Tales
Ghost Hunter's Guide to Haunted Ohio - Over 25 NEW, terrifying
    stories
The Wright Stuff: A Guide to Life in the Dayton Area

See the last page of the book for how to order your own copy of
this book or other books by Chris Woodyard

Copyright @ 1994 Chris Woodyard

All rights reserved. No part of this book may be reproduced or
transmitted in any form or by any means, electronic or mechanical,
including photocopying, recording, or by any informational storage or
retrieval system—except by a reviewer who may quote brief passages
in a review to be printed in a magazine, newspaper, or electronic
media—without permission in writing from the publisher. For
information contact Kestrel Publications, 1811 Stonewood Drive,
Dayton, OH 45432-4002, (937) 426-5110, invisiblei@aol.com.

Fifth Printing 2007
Printed in the United States of America
Typesetting by Copy Plus, Dayton, OH
Cover Art by Larry Hensel, Hensel Graphics, Xenia, OH
Library of Congress Catalog Card Number: 91-75343

Woodyard, Chris
Haunted Ohio III: Still More Ghostly Tales from the Buckeye State/
Chris Woodyard
SUMMARY: Ghostly tales, true and traditional, from around Ohio.

ISBN: 0-962847224
1. Ghost Stories —United States—Ohio
2. Ghosts—United States—Ohio
3. Haunted Houses—United States—Ohio
I. Woodyard, Chris II. Title
398.25 W912H
070.593 Wo
Z1033.L73

For Anne, Katy, Rosi, and Sarah—the Four Fates

ACKNOWLEDGMENTS

Many people have contributed their stories and their support to *Haunted Ohio III.* In particular I want to thank the following: R.J. Abraham; Dorothy Philips Amling; "Anonymous;" "Dr. Ron Archer;" Joanne Baccani; Janice Barry; Eric Beach; Jim Beard; Michael Berger; Glenna Berres; Jim Blount; Joseph R.Blum; Margery Brissey; Christine Budich; Dale Bugos; Dale Bundy; John Campbell; Carol Carey; Bernard L. Carpenter; Carl Cassavecchia; Stacey Christopher; Bonnie Collins; Dorothy Cox; George Crout; Richard Crawford; Dennis Dalton; Nadine Daugherty; Jeff Diess; LaVonne & Mike Dotter; Barbara Dreimiller; Becky Edwards; Dale Edwards; Elizabeth & Shirley Ellis; Lisa Fatzinger; Greg Feketik; Charles Flick; Vivian Flynt; Martha S. Foster; Phyllis Frederick; Audrey Gilbert; Melinda Gilpin; Holli Gomez; Penny Gompf; Janet Goode; Betty Grabill; Angela R. Granata; Rose Greene; Sandra J. Grinder; Nancy Hamilton; Rick Hamm; Mrs. Helen M. Hansen; Carol Harbaugh; Joyce Harvey; Rich Heileman; Anita Henderson; Ursula Hertenstein; W.W. Higgins; Bob & Judy Hilton; Pat Hindenach; James Hodulik; Alan D. Hopewell; the Rev. Gerald Hunter; Jennifer Imel; Carol Ivers; Lesly Kalbfleisch; Judy Key; Wanda Kirby; Erwin & Dorothy S. Klein; Gale LaPointe; Dawn Marie Leigh; Pat Lillie; Littleton Funeral Home; Jo Ann Leonhard; Art Lofredo; Audrey M. Mackiewicz; Jan Materni; Patty Mason; Charlotte Matthews; Lee McCool; Martha Mechel; Merry Go Round Museum; Rosalie Moore; Jennifer Moorhead; Amy Mundhenk; Hank Nest; Roberta Oelker; Gwen Ohlinger; Tammy Park; Peggy & Tom Parker; Troi & David Penwell; Lloyd & Marilyn Petry; Phyllis Powell; Regie Powell; Lemoine Rice; Ross County Historical Society; Beverly Rountree; Roger W. Russell; St. Paris Public Library; Marilyn Saurer; Tish Scarmuzzi; Mrs. Toni Seiler; Janet Senne; Mrs. Elizabeth Sharp; Judy Smith; Karen Sobul; James Stalter; Michael Stuz; Debbie Trimbach; Elaine Vanderschrier; Rick VanLandingham III; Victor Vick; Angie Waryne; B.J. Wells; G. Patrick Weston; Brian A. Williams; Jay A. With; Toni Wolcott; Nanette Young; Lois Zizert; Chris Zychowski; and of course the inimitable staff of the Beavercreek Library, whose circulation I singlehandedly tripled, especially Ann Diener, Jo Ellen Fannin, Susan Griffin, and Toni White. A special thanks goes to Curt Dalton, researcher extraordinaire who deserved hazardous duty pay for his labors.

TABLE OF CONTENTS

Introduction

Prelude: The Flames

INTRODUCTION

Go away, live people, stop haunting the dead...
-Kenneth Fearing-

Ghosts scare me. They always have and they probably always will. I *know* logically that they can't harm me, that most of them are just lost souls, tired and unable to find their way home. I *ought* to feel sorry for them. But I'm afraid just the same....

I've tried to explain this to well-meaning spiritualists and channelers who believe that, if I only understood about ghosts, I wouldn't be afraid. Understanding and logic have nothing to do with it—it is a purely physical reaction: my adrenalin rises, my breath is shortened, my blood chilled. I've compared it to a dog who howls in pain at the whistle humans cannot hear. I feel something most people do not and it deranges my nervous system. I do not seem to be able to control it, any more than I can control sweating in the heat, or shivering in the cold.

In 1993 I began to see ghosts again. As I said in *Haunted Ohio*, I learned to block them out when I was young because they scared me too much. I've dealt with a lot of old fears recently; it is almost as if, by unblocking old paths of thinking, I was unblocking that window into the other world. That may be the good news.

The bad news is that a large box of readers' letters and stories have vanished. I figured it would turn up somewhere. It hasn't.

The phantom cabin at Ft. Amanda, the gas-flame blue ghost at Dayton, the haunted group-home in Jackson, and so many more I can't remember them—all lost. So to those who shared your letters and stories, my deepest apologies. Perhaps, when the cosmic prankster decides to return them, I'll have to write *Haunted Ohio 13: The Lost Tales.*

My goal was to have at least one story from each county. To my astonishment, I've failed. Although I visited, wrote libraries, historical societies, sent researchers, and appealed for stories in local newspapers, there still remain "dead zones"—counties without stories—for the moment.

If your story didn't make it into print, please don't be upset: I received an incredible number of stories. Perhaps your tale will make a future edition. And I have plans for *The Complete Haunted Ohio*, with photographs.

Before we get into the body of the book, let me say a word about ouija boards. People often ask me if I use one. I do not and I don't recommend them for anyone. They only attract lying, earthbound spirits who will first tell you truths, then entangle you in lies. Imagine that you lived in an apartment in New York City and you walked out the door, grabbed the first person you saw, and brought them into your home. You're doing exactly the same thing—only riskier—when you call up just any old entity on the ethernet.

Use a little common sense: Is your grandmother who is supposed to be enjoying the bliss of Heaven, going to return to push around a little plastic pointer for a bunch of giggling teenagers at a slumber party? I don't think so. Just stay away from ouija boards, they are not a game and they'll do you no good.

In all my travels, I've been terrified to find out just how many ghosts inhabit Ohio. These Buckeye ghosts just won't stay buried. So now sit back, put your back to the wall, read 'em—and creep....

NOTE: Names with one asterisk mean that the name was changed 1) by request of the person involved or 2) because I couldn't find the person and ask permission to use their real name. If you are one of these persons and are surprised to see your story here, please contact me.

THE FLAMES

Like a pale martyr in his shirt of fire.
-Alexander Smith-

Nursing her egg-nog and listening to her boss tell the same stories he told at every office Christmas party, Cindy* heard the doorbell ring. From her spot in the kitchen she saw her hostess open the door to Brett*, one of her co-workers. As he walked into the hallway, Cindy stared in horror. Brett's body was wreathed in flames; his face distorted with the rising heat and smoke.

How could he catch on fire just walking through the door? she thought wildly. Then he strolled into the kitchen, smiling, and Cindy saw his bright red sweater. She broke into a cold sweat of relief. The fire surrounding him had looked so real.... She wondered if someone had spiked the egg-nog.

Later in the evening she saw Brett standing with his arm up on the mantelpiece. His head was thrown back; his mouth open in agony. His body was shrouded in bright red-orange flames. Then Cindy heard him laugh and the flames dwindled into the red sweater. Just a reflection of the real fire, she thought, struggling to make sense of it.

But would that explain the dark shadows like patches of charring on his face? Or the greasy burnt smell hanging in her nostrils? Once, brushing up against him, she felt the intense heat coming off his arm. Cindy left the party early with a headache.

She still had the headache when she turned on the news the next morning. She saw oily black smoke rolling up out of a familiar building—the factory where she worked. Then a white-shrouded body being carried out to an ambulance. Under the sheet, she imagined the twisted, blackened limbs. She turned up the sound. A photo was flashed on the screen: It was Brett, who had been burned to death, the victim of an explosion.[1]

HOME IS WHERE THE HAUNT IS
Ghosts around the house

All houses wherein men have lived and died
Are haunted houses.
-Henry Wadsworth Longfellow-

THE BIG CHILL

Everybody knew she was crazy. She'd walk down the
street in the middle of August wearing four layers of sweaters
and that filthy brown coat. Sweat would be running down her
face from under her matted hair and grey knit hat, but she'd
complain about how cold she was. And then she'd start to
swear—not at you, but at something just above your head and a
little to the left. You would mumble an excuse about remem-
bering an appointment and edge away. She might stare after
you and then stump off with her painful, rolling walk, cursing
at the birds, swatting at invisible snowflakes.

Nobody was much surprised when she froze to death
during a hard winter in 1979. She hadn't paid her gas bill for
months—half the time, her mail lay unopened on the porch.
The utility company gave her every chance, but finally cut off
the gas in the early summer. She never got around to asking
them to turn it back on when the weather turned cold.

She was found frozen to death in the Darst Avenue house
in Dayton, her body shrouded in layers of clothes so that she
looked like a walrus lying there, all blue-grey and glassy-eyed.

Jeff knew nothing of this when he bought the house in the
early fall of 1990. But as soon as the weather turned chilly,
something peculiar happened.

"The cover of the furnace repeatedly fell off," Jeff said. "The first time it happened, we didn't know that the furnace wouldn't operate if it was off. So the house got freezing cold. Finally I bent the edges of the metal cover so you had to pound it to get it back on. It still came off. I didn't understand it. It was on there tight! And it only happened in the middle of the night. You'd wake up freezing."

Jeff found out about the dead woman at a block party two days before Halloween, 1990.

"The woman who used to live in my house was an alcoholic who ended up drinking rubbing alcohol. That final winter, a young girl came to visit and found her there frozen."

A couple of months after buying the house, Jeff and his wife separated. He kept the house and the furnace cover stopped falling off. Then one night, he felt someone in his bed. "I woke up one night, lying on my right shoulder. And I felt somebody behind me. Like someone had thrown an arm over me, just cuddling up. I was half asleep, and I was terrified. I wanted to scream out for help. I tried to roll over and reach the phone, but I couldn't! If it was a dream, I've never had a dream like that in my life. I hadn't been drinking—I hadn't eaten any spicy chili!

"About a week later, the furnace cover fell off again in the middle of the night. And a week or so after that, the arm came back, just resting on me. That's when I started thinking, 'I'm not dreaming.'

"A few days later, I sat my little boy in front of the TV and went down to the basement to bring the laundry up to fold. I heard him walking around the kitchen. I had something on the stove and was afraid he'd burn himself so I called to him to sit on the basement steps. He came and sat. And as I was turning off the light to the basement, he said to me, 'Daddy, whose eyes are those?'

'What eyes?'

'Daddy, whose eyes are those?' he repeated. Then he said, 'Oh, never mind, they belong to that guy behind you.'

"I didn't look behind me so I don't know what he saw! My son is a very smart three-year old, but he's not a fantasizer. He doesn't have imaginary friends or anything. And he calls anybody—man or woman—'guy.'"

In May, 1994 I called Jeff for an update.

"Just yesterday, the sixteenth, I felt the arm again. I know somebody's there and I can't move. Last night I kept shaking it off and it kept happening over and over again: I was lying on my back. And somebody was holding my arms by the wrists."

Jeff has tried to make his home warm and welcoming. But something of the chill of the grave still hangs over it: a woman's frozen spirit seeking the warmth of human flesh.

THE PHANTOM MANSION

In October of 1980, 12-year-old Jay and a friend were scouring the old Myers Lake Park in Stark County for collect-ible beer cans. They noticed a small cabin where they found a rare bottle-neck beer can. Something about the place spooked them, so, clutching their prize, they left the cabin and began investigating the surrounding woods.

They found a path with trees growing in a row on either side like a tunnel and followed it until it opened into a court-yard decorated with shrubs and a marble circle. In the distance the two boys saw a grand old house, bigger than anything they had ever imagined. Thinking they had stumbled on the remains of the Meyers Lake mansion, which had burned down years before, they walked up to the house. As they got closer, they saw smoke rising from the chimney. Suddenly a frail-looking woman dressed in a white gown appeared in a window.

That was enough for the boys who ran for it. After a bit, they regained their courage and decided to go back and investigate. It took several hours of stamping around in the woods before they found the tunnel of trees and the clearing. There Jay found an empty matchbook advertising the Meyers Lake Resort Hotel. In the courtyard they found the marble circle and the rare beer can they had dropped in their flight. The only thing missing was the mansion...

Jay and his friend have made many trips to the area, which is now built over, but they have never seen the house again. Jay wrote, "I am saddened by the new construction in the area because I may never know the truth about the house we saw. The only material things I have to prove I was there are a beer can and a pack of matches. The question I have is, did my friend and I look into the past or was it some sort of ghost house?"

THE POSSESSIVE GHOST

Mary* lived in Chesapeake, a small Lawrence County community on the Ohio River. She seemed like a regular housewife with a husband and two children, but she was a powerful psychic. You couldn't lie to her about where you'd been: she knew instantly. She drove her family to distraction by knowing the contents of wrapped gifts. Yet when she told her family she was dying, they thought she was just looking for some attention.

By the time the family realized Mary had cancer, it was too late. On her deathbed Mary warned her husband Dan* that if he ever brought another woman into her home, she would haunt him. Again, no one took this seriously, although she *was* unusually fond of her house. After Mary died in October of 1986, Dan remarried and moved out of Ohio.

The next summer he brought his wife Kay* back to Chesapeake to visit Spencer* his son who had moved into Mary's house after his father's marriage. After chatting a bit, Kay went into the bathroom. Suddenly father and son were startled to hear her screaming for help. They rushed to the door, only to find that, while the doorknob turned and the key moved in the lock, the door stayed firmly shut. Kay had claustrophobia and Dan was frantic. Spencer went for tools to take the door off its hinges. Then the two men realized: Mary. Dan closed his eyes and whispered, "All right, Mary. That's enough." At that, the door opened.

Dan died in 1989. In July, 1990 Spencer brought his own bride to the Chesapeake house. He never gave a thought to his mother's warning. But his wife Ellen* was immediately spooked by a pair of "invisible hands" pushing her out of the house. Doors flew open; brand-new light bulbs exploded. When Ellen saw "something" in the guest room closet, she moved out—just three months after their marriage. Spencer wondered bitterly if his mother was satisfied.

Spencer fell on hard times and was forced to sell the house. After returning from the closing, he found an owl music box of Mary's on the floor, smashed into a thousand pieces.

As of this writing, Spencer is still living in the house, renting it from the man who bought it. So far, various strange twists of fate have stymied his attempts to buy another house. After Ellen's departure, the house began a sudden decay: the bedroom floor sagged, the sewer backed up under the house, the garage roof fell to pieces, and, most sinister of all, rats infested the house.

On three separate occasions, Spencer has found broken panes of glass in the kitchen door and window. He first blamed his dogs, but then realized they would have had to have climbed into the sink to break the window. A burglar? The glass was broken *outwards*, struck from the inside.

At least once a month Spencer has the same dream: he dreams of loading his belongings into a battered U-Haul®, pulling out onto the little street in front of his home and stopping for one last look at the old family place—only to see a thick column of black smoke rolling from the upstairs window—sparked by the white-hot anger of a possessive ghost.

THE FATHER WHO COULD NOT REST

One afternoon in the summer of 1993 I got a call from a woman. She sounded nervous. People who call me often are.

"I think I have a ghost..." she began hesitantly.

"Stop right there," I said. "If you want me to visit, I don't want to hear anything about it."

I may have sounded abrupt, but if I can, I like to go into a house without any information so I can sense for myself where the ghost is and what it wants.

So I made an appointment to visit along with Rosi Mackey and Anne Oscard. And, due to a last-minute babysitting glitch, my daughter was also with us.

As we drove up Rt. 49 in Dayton, Anne said, "This is very close to my old neighborhood, where I grew up. There was a haunted house just around the corner and I can remember running past it with my friends, hoping the ghost wouldn't catch us."

We turned onto a little side street off Seibenthaler.

"This is very strange," said Anne, "My old house is just around the corner—and *there's the haunted house!*"

It was a ramshackle frame farmhouse painted a spotty grey with a barn on the hill behind it, covered with vines, and overshadowed by a tangle of trees. If ever a house looked haunted, this was it. I looked at the address I'd been given. The house we were visiting was next door.

That house had a perky lift to its roofline, and colorful flowers in the yard. Inside, the house was filled with cheerful country touches: wreaths, candles, and spongeware.

Children peered at us from around the corner as Debbie greeted us in her calico jumper with a heart applique. "I run an after-school daycare," she explained.

She let us have the run of the house. We fanned out with our notebooks. I was drawn irresistibly up the stairs where someone invisible stood in the back hall and, in the last bedroom, a folding closet door abruptly opened by itself.

Downstairs in the family room, I halted at the doors. There was a sharp pain in my hip. I felt a male presence strongly in one corner and, in the bathroom, the air was damp as if someone had recently showered in there. The towels were dry.

Afterwards we all gathered in the dining room to talk things over. "I saw several cats in the living room," Anne began. "I thought they were real until I saw the way the living cats didn't react to them."

Debbie's eyes filled with tears. "We lost two cats to

leukemia just 6 months ago," she said. "And that's about when all of this started."

Anne continued, "I also saw an elderly man and woman sitting on the couch in the living room, holding hands. They looked so happy together!"

"That would have been my parents," said Debbie sadly. "Until my mother died, they were inseparable." And she told us that when her mother had died 14 years before, her father had moved in with them. They built the "family room" on the back of the house just for him. The old gentleman developed cancer and had died at the house about 6 months before our visit.

Various things had been going on: As she walked up the stairs, Debbie felt a wind brush by her arm. "Dad, is that you?" she blurted. Her mother-in-law heard someone walking down the upstairs hall when everyone else was gone. Debbie's son's friends have smelled BenGay® in the bathroom. The TV stations change mysteriously. Debbie has seen the door to the family room move on its own, as if somebody had pushed through it.

In April, 1993, the family returned from an outing to find all of the clocks reset 15 minutes ahead of time.

"I have a tendency to run late," Debbie admitted. "And Dad always moved the clocks ahead."

All of us sensed an older man in the back family room. As for the corner where I felt the man, "That was where we had Dad's bed. He died there," Debbie explained. "The night that he died, my oldest son woke up in a cold sweat. He had been very close to his Grandmother and he told me she had come and said to him, 'I'm taking Grandpa with me.'

"Within an hour, my father passed on. I know she was calling him. He was looking up at the ceiling and reaching out for someone."

Debbie told us that her brothers were much older, so, in effect, she had been an only child. She missed her parents painfully and we speculated that her father was staying on in the house to make sure she was all right.

Suddenly my daughter spoke up.

"Did your father have a bald spot and a big white handle-bar mustache?"

Puzzled, Debbie said, "Yes."

"Did he walk with a carved, polished brown wood cane?"

"Yes, he did. The cancer got into the bone. I nearly buried him with that cane."

"Did he like soap operas?"

"He loved them! He'd lie on that couch in the family room and watch them for hours."

By now the hair on my arms was standing up.

"Was this his favorite chair I'm sitting in?"

"Yes. How do you know these things?"

The little girl was apologetic, "He's standing over there in the hall telling me."

As a final ghostly flourish, as we walked out to our car, Anne told Debbie how the house next door had frightened her as she was growing up. I remarked that it looked like the original farmhouse in the plat, complete with surviving barn.

"Barn?" said Debbie, puzzled. "There used to be a barn there, but we had it torn it down because it was dangerous. The only thing holding it up was the vines."

"Tore it down? 15 minutes ago?" I thought to myself, but I walked around to where I could see the hill behind the house. The barn I had seen when we drove up wasn't there any more.

DREAM HOUSES

One of the oldest chestnuts in 19th-century ghost literature is the story about the woman who dreams nightly of a beautiful house. One day, out in the country, she sees the same house and finds that it is for sale. On making inquiries, she finds that the house is haunted—by her, says the caretaker.

Here are two similar stories, only these happen to be true...

Pat had a recurring dream about a house since she was ten. In her dream, she was showing people around the house. She would walk up a stairway into a turret and, looking to the left, she would see a stained glass window. Upstairs, there were four-poster beds in all the rooms. But one of the doors terrified her. She could never open that door.

During the summer of 1993 Pat found a picture of her Hancock County dream house for sale. "A friend, her daughter, and I went to look at the house. When I saw it, I was filled with an overwhelming sadness. A lot of the things in the house were just as I had seen them in my dream: the layout was the same; a railroad track ran out back; upstairs in the attic hall was a copper-lined cistern. The bedrooms even had four-poster beds. But just as I got to one of the bedroom doors, I felt electricity and I couldn't open the door. My friend had to do it. I felt like I was going to scream. I was shaking. Behind that door was the attic where we found a four-poster bed. There was an electric feeling in the attic. I was terrified, but I felt I had to explore the room." Pat wonders if she maybe lived—or died— there before.

Rosi Mackey, my ghost-hunting friend, had a recurring dream from her earliest years: "I'm going upstairs in an old house. In my dream, I know I've been here before. I see old-fashioned poster beds, antique dressers, old pictures. I know nobody lives here, but there is no dust. Somebody is taking of the place, but I don't know why. At the end of the hall on a table is a turn-of-the-century wedding picture in a frame.

"I talked about this dream over the years to many people, including my husband Steve before we got married. After 12 years of marriage, Steve's father moved to West Lafayette, a town I'd never visited, with his new wife, who took us to visit her father's house.

"It came to me as I was rounding the bend of the stair: This was the house. There were the bedrooms, the furniture, the wedding photo. The house had not been occupied for about a year, since her father was ill and staying with her sister. But someone came in to take care of it. I finally understood why my dream house was empty, although cared for. But I still don't know why I dreamed of it for so many years...."

MERLE THE GHOST

"The real estate woman jokingly said to us, 'You know, this house is haunted.' My husband said, 'If you can document that, I'll pay extra.' Now it's dormant," Barb* commented. "But things constantly happened that we had no explanation for. Objects seemed to move magically from one room to another, with me alone in the house.

"The ghost particularly loved to hide the baby's pacifier. It was almost an obsession! My husband Mike* would search all over the house and finally walk up to the drugstore to get a new one. When he went in to lay the baby down, he'd find the old pacifier in the middle of her floor.

"We had lots of fun with the lights. When we went out in the evenings, leaving only the kitchen and back porch light on, every light in the house would be on when we returned, including the ones in the attic and basement.

"One night we decided to get creative. We turned all lights on *except* for the attic and basement. When we came back, the house was pitch black.

"As I stood at the stove, I got cold chills for a few seconds like something had walked through me, then left again, and I could feel the heat from the stove.

"After we moved in, I was working on a card table in the kitchen. There were boxes all over the kitchen. Several coats were piled neatly on one stack of boxes.

"I saw a motion to my left, looked, and saw the coats standing straight up in the air—as if someone had picked them up—then they dropped 5 feet away from the base of the pile of boxes.

"One day I was sitting on the steps, cleaning the banister. Just then, the front door opened as if someone was going to walk through. The door stopped dead in mid-swing, stood there for a few seconds, then shut again—exactly the rhythm of someone coming in the door. I made light of it and called to Mike, 'Oh, honey, the ghost is home!' He dismissed it since it was a windy day. But if the wind had caught the door, it would have slammed against the wall instead of stopping cold.

"One evening as I walked into my daughter's bedroom and switched on the lights, I saw a large book lying open on the floor. Instantly the book slammed shut, cover and all. Almost as if I had walked in on him and caught him in the act.

"I say 'he' because we know the ghost is a male. The legend went that a young boy living here drowned and they never found the body. I got curious and sat down with with a neighbor who happened to be the original owner's niece.

"We think the ghost is Merle Breneiser. He had Hodgkin's disease and his parents, William and Bertha, bought the house in the 1920s for him when he was thirteen because he loved it. He died in the hospital a year after the house was moved to Fairborn from Osborne.

"It makes sense: all the things with lights; playing little hide-and-seek games. Once he took a screwdriver right out of my pocket. I was taking down the old curtain rods and couldn't quite reach one. So I put the screwdriver in my back pocket and went to get a chair. I came back, and the screwdriver was gone. I searched all over the first floor and found it in the middle of the kitchen counter.

"Our neighbor showed me a photo of Merle. The minute I laid eyes on the picture, it was *deja vu.* Maybe I dreamed him. He was very handsome—dark hair parted on the left, swooping over his forehead, brown eyes, a very boyish face with a square jaw and straight nose. A very cute boy. He was wearing a black jacket with a white shirt and string tie.

"When my daughter was about two years old, I was sitting in the living room reading, when I heard somebody crying. 'Oh,' I thought, "my daughter is awake!' She was sound asleep. I still heard someone sobbing and crying. I checked again; she was still asleep. You could hear it best in the living room. I know a previous owner actually knocked a hole at the back of the fireplace trying to find the crying ghost.

"It's been very quiet lately, almost as if the noise of the renovation stirred him up and now he's settled down. He's never hurt anybody and he's lots of fun!"

THE LADY IN BROWN

Troi and David Penwell have lived in not one, but two haunted houses in Washington Court House. They moved into their 1890s Columbus Avenue house in February 1988.

"The very first month something unusual happened. David was playing the piano—he loves old sheet music, Hoagy Carmichael, that sort of thing—when the phone rang. He answered it and someone said, 'I really liked that last song you played, play it again.' It was a rather gruff voice, like an older person, more female than male."

Unnerved, David called his wife at work. She heard the fear in his voice and went home. Together, they searched for an explanation. It was still cold and no windows were open. Troi even walked around the house.

"Someone might have been able to see him through the sheer curtains at the window. We thought maybe one of the kids at our church did it. But pranksters like to know they got to you and nobody ever asked us if they'd scared us with that phone call."

"So what did you do when you got the call?" I asked David.

"I played the song again!"

Sometimes a sweet flowery perfume would waft by Troi who could never locate the source. Twice David and Troi heard a crash as if the large glass picture window in the sunroom had shattered, but they never found out what caused the sound.

David began calling the presence "Marie" after a former owner of the house. After their daughter was born prematurely he heard footsteps pacing in their daughter's room as if Marie were watching over the child.

Christmas, 1989, David told Troi's aunt about some of the mysterious manifestations. Not wanting to frighten her aunt, Troi tried to downplay the situation, "Oh, David, you're always saying stuff like this, there's no other woman running around this house!"

At that, the light behind the couch blinked and went off. Ten seconds later the ceiling light blinked and went off. Another ten seconds later the Christmas tree lights blinked and went off. All other lights in the house stayed on. And a few moments later all the darkened lights went back on.

Despite Marie, Troi was happy in the house. But when her husband fell in love with a bigger, cheaper house with three stories and crystal chandeliers, she was tempted by the thought of staying home with her young child. So she gave in.

The Penwells were in their new house for two months before 18-month-old Katy began to wake up every night, pointing in the corner of her room and crying as if she saw something horrible. Troi went into the child's room and faced the corner.

"I said, 'I don't know who you are; you're welcome to stay as long as you're not interfering with us. And right now you're scaring my child. I want it stopped. Now.' I was very firm. It was that mother instinct coming out. But it stopped. She didn't wake up that night or any night since. But she still sees things I can't."

A few months later Troi was standing in the downstairs bathroom when a woman walked past the door. She was middle-aged and wore a long dress, which Troi identified as late 1800s by the style. It was a dark color—black or brown, with lace around the collar and the three-quarter-length sleeves. It had a little train and a bustle. Her hair was swept up, but her face was already past the doorframe by the time Troi looked.

Two months later, David saw the same woman in the dining room. Three months after David, Troi's mother saw her.

"Ironically we were watching the movie *Ghost*. My mom looked up and saw the lady go from the parlor to the hallway."

When David went up to the second floor to get Christmas decorations in 1991, he came back down white as a sheet and refused to go back up by himself. Something had tapped him on the shoulder very firmly. Sort of a "What are you doing up here?" tap.

Troi was painting late one night. "I was tired and suddenly I felt something—it felt like a hand, laid on my shoulder. I almost felt like someone was saying, 'Oh, God love you, you're working so hard!' It was very soothing."

David thinks the female ghost is Alice Rettig whose husband built the house in 1884. A neighbor showed them a picture of Alice standing on the lawn with children all around her. One of the children may also haunt the house.

On a hot night in August, 1991 Troi woke to find the bed moving. She looked over at David and could see the sheet over him moving as if someone were plunging fists into his arm and side.

Troi wonders if the invisible creature was a child, playing rough. "I dreamed of a boy around seven years old, dressed in knickers and high stockings," said Troi. He was standing in the hall, then he walked into the room, and stood at the foot of the bed. I was very frightened of this child—there was an evil around him. In my dream I tried to wake up David and I couldn't. I remember being so terribly frightened that I said to the child, 'In the name of the Lord Jesus Christ, what do you want?'"

At that she woke up. David was still asleep beside her. But she was so terrified that it took her several months to get over it. She thinks the ghost is still in the house, "but he's at bay."

In January of 1992 at 2:30 a.m. Troi again woke to find their bed moving. It was a methodical bounce, like someone standing at the foot of the bed deliberately pushing on the mattress. First she thought David was kicking something in his sleep. Then she wondered if Katy was in their bed. As soon as she looked up, it stopped. An hour later, a frightened Katy came scrambling into bed. As David and Troi discussed the jolting bed, Katy suddenly awoke and told them about "a man" bouncing a ball all over her toys and room and her parents' bed.

Finally Troi said to the ghost, "Look, I understand you've been here a lot longer than I have, but this is my home. There is no reason for our worlds to collide. You can exist here without us hearing you, seeing you, or in any way knowing you're here and I'd like to keep it that way." It seemed to work. Nothing has happened since January 1992.

"We're not trying to run anything out of here. I'm not trying to dictate to them. I just don't want them to be interfering with us. I don't want to be frightened; I don't want my daughter to be frightened. If we can mutually show respect for each other, we'll be fine."

GRANDPAPPY

The delightful Martha Foster, now of Athens, graciously shared her story of "Grandpappy," the ghost whose home she borrowed in Gallipolis:

My husband, our children and I, newcomers to Gallipolis, had been living in Grandpappy's house for several weeks before we realized it was his; having bought it, we had supposed it ours.

It was a large, old-fashioned slate-roofed farmhouse facing the Ohio River near Gallipolis. It suited us perfectly. All it needed was central heat, running water, electricity, fresh plaster, a kitchen sink, its termites eradicated, a bathroom installed, its several chimneys rebuilt or relined, its walnut woodwork and sunny pine floors scraped free of paint, its outside painted and its shutters removed from the haymow, mended, painted and mounted. It was with the coming of those who attended to such matters that we began to suspect that the house was not ours.

"Seen any spooks yet?" the plumber asked.

"No, should we?"

The plumber looked at the carpenter.

"There are them as does, Ma'am," the carpenter said.

"Well, we haven't," my husband said, "A dog on the hill back there howls all night—maybe he keeps them away."

"Not that dog; he's been howling for fifty, sixty year."

"Remarkable!"

Seeming to detect the skepticism in my husband's voice the plumber said earnestly, "Doc, that dog ain't no ordinary dog. That dog a ha'nt. He's out there lookin' for the old man."

"Looking' in the wrong place," the carpenter said, jerking a knowing thumb toward the stair. "Old man's up there."

We did not pursue the subject—we were paying the plumber and the carpenter by the hour.

Then the plasterer came. "Won't do no good tryin' to plaster that corner room upstairs," he said. "Plaster won't stick. Never has since the old man died; he don't want it tetched."

"Tetch it anyway," my husband said.

The plasterer did his best. Once his loaded mortarboard was wrenched from his hand and propelled through an open window, and twice, his scaffolding fell with him on it, but eventually the room was plastered. "Reckon he's give up," the plasterer said as he rolled up the canvas with which he had protected the floor.

That night, with a roar that awakened the baby, delighted the two boys and dismayed my husband and me, the entire ceiling tumbled down onto the bare floor. After two more tries the plaster stayed in place, but we waited six weeks before calling a paperhanger.

The paperhanger clucked his tongue and said, "Wouldn't mess with that room if I was you, Doc. The old man, he don't want it tetched."

"Tetch it anyway."

"Well, if you say so."

The paperhanger's scaffolding collapsed; his bucket of paste upset into his lunch; and while he was cleaning it up, three strips of wallpaper swooped down from the ceiling and wrapped themselves about his head. Nevertheless he persisted; the room was papered.

For all the disturbances he made, Grandpappy seemed careful not to let members of our family see him, although he several times appeared to other people. His most prolonged appearance was during his favorite time of late afternoon, on a

day when neither my husband nor I was at home. Jenny and
the children were in the hall watching a cabinet-maker and his
father carry upstairs a wardrobe we had ordered. The father
was visiting his son from another state. He had not heard of
"the old man" nor met any of our family.

The wardrobe was heavy. When the son, who was in the
rear, dropped a corner of it onto his fingers and let out a healthy
oath, the father said sharply, "Watch your language!" After
they had reached the upper hall he said, "The doctor didn't like
what you said back there."

"What do you mean?"

"Didn't you hear him? He said, 'Don't ever use that kind
of language in front of the children!' You must have seen
him—he was standing right over there by the railing. Watched
us until we were all the way up, then he went back to his
room."

"Wasn't Doc," Jenny said, "He ain't here."

"Your grandfather?"

"Oh, no, just our ghost."

With two little boys and a young baby to care for and a
beautiful house to keep, I had little time to think about
"ha'nts," but one day when a taxi driver remarked, "You the
ones bought the old Bailey place, ain't you? Seen anything of
the old man?"

I asked what old man.

"Talk to Miss Janet," he said, "Miss Janet Bailey. She can
tell you."

Miss Janet was a charming elderly spinster, a graduate of
Julliard School of Music, and our son Chip's piano teacher.
"They're talking about my grandfather," she said. "I wondered
when you'd ask. He built that house well over a hundred years
ago and lived in it the rest of his life—and ever since. I was
brought up there by him and Grandmother. They helped me
through the School—Grandfather loved music. He was
difficult in some ways, but I adored him. He died the summer
after I graduated—a very painful death. He had a bench in the

pasture hill back of the house where he liked to go and take a nap, or just sit. His dog always went along, for companionship and to keep an eye on a bull that was in the pasture, though the bull was a gentle one. One day while Grandfather slept, a hunter's stray bullet struck and killed the dog, exciting the bull. The bull charged Grandfather, goring him so severely that after lying for weeks in that corner room upstairs, he died of his wounds, fighting all the way. Until the very end, at night when he thought everyone was asleep, he would drag himself out of bed and hobble down the hall with his walking stick. After he died, we still heard him—heard the tap-tap of his walking stick. Once I tried to spy on him. The minute I opened the door into the hall, the walking stick landed at my feet with a clatter, as if thrown there."

Miss Janet laughed. "Grandfather had a temper all right, and it stayed with him. He and Grandmother had slept in a four-poster without a canopy. Grandmother liked canopies, and the bed had a frame for one, but Grandfather told her no such effeminate truck was going his bed; she could choose between sleeping under a canopy or sleeping with him. At a decent interval after his death Grandmother asked me to help her tack the canopy onto its frame. 'No sense now keeping it in the blanket chest,' she said. Shortly after fastening the canopy to its frame, we returned to the room only to find the frame as bare as a plucked turkey. The canopy was wadded into a corner, the tacks lying points up on the floor. Without a word Grandmother picked up the tacks, folded the canopy and put it in the blanket chest."

I grew more and more irritated that that Grandpappy appeared to strangers but not to us, and especially not to me, perhaps his truest friend. One late afternoon, hearing his footsteps returning down the hall at the end of their usual routine I followed them. "It's not fair!" I shouted at the sound receding up the stair. "You're cranky, stiff-necked and ungrateful!"

Whether scolding did it, I don't know, but the next day, for the first and only time Grandpappy let me see him. The afternoon was sunny and tranquil. I was seated in the study, which opened off the hall near the bottom of the stairs; I was reading and listening to Chip as he practiced the piano around the corner in the hall....For some reason I looked up from my book and saw him standing in the doorway. He was half turned away from me, leaning against the doorjamb and looking down at Chip as though taking pleasure in watching him play and in listening to the not-always-musical notes he was making.

Grandpappy was tall, thin, slightly stooped. He was wearing dark, rather baggy trousers; I could see where his suspenders crossed in the back over what appeared to be long-sleeved underwear. His hair was gray, smooth and rather long; his profile, which was all I could see of his face, was firm, angular, and beardless. Even as I was looking at him, he dissolved before my eyes, although I felt he was still there, enjoying himself very much. Later I described him to Miss Janet, "That was Grandfather, all right," she said.[1]

A CRY IN THE NIGHT

Karen of Columbus solved the problem of things going "waaah" in the night in a unique and practical way:

For several years in the early 1980s my friend T.A. and I, along with my 6-month old daughter shared an old row house on Indianola near Hudson St. While sitting in the living room, usually at night, you could hear a baby crying.

Being a relatively new mother, I was very attuned to the pitch of my daughter's cry and I would run upstairs to take care of her. There she would be, peacefully asleep. After many incidents of this kind we figured that there must be another baby living close by. There were no buildings front or rear; none of the neighbors had small children. We began to wonder where the noise was coming from.

This happened so often that we learned to wait a few minutes before checking on my daughter because we got so we could distinguish between her cry and the ghost baby's! This even happened once during a party where the people sitting on the upstairs steps all heard the ghost cry. It didn't worry us— we just felt that it was some leftover energy kicked up by all the antiques we owned and by our willingness to listen— remember, this was a row house that had probably had hundreds of tenants. You can't always move everything when you leave...

This only became a problem when it started waking me up at night several times a week. I knew that if I was to get a good night's sleep, I had to figure out how to stop it. The next time it woke me up, I sat up in bed, shook myself to ensure that I was awake and checked on my daughter whose crib was in my room. She was fast asleep and I could still hear the crying.

I summoned up my nerve, got up, and went in search of the sound. My only reservation was that I was *not* going into the basement—I'm not that brave! I went into the hallway. The baby sounded like it was right in my roommate's bedroom. I opened the door and my roommate lay asleep in his bed, oblivious to the noise. I was surprised and a little scared, but, in my best "motherly" voice, I cooed to the "baby" as I did to my own daughter, talking gently and quietly. Almost immediately, the crying quieted down and then it was gone. I was awakened only once more and did the same thing without getting out of bed. We never heard the crying again.

THE SMOKY GHOST

The young mother worked nights as a nurse, and sometimes she was still asleep when her third-grade daughter came home from school. One day, the mother left some trash burning in the back yard. Poking curiously at the fire, her daughter caught her her hair on fire. She ran to the door and pounded to get in, but her mother could not hear her. The child panicked and ran down the street, her movement fanning the flames. Her mother slept on, not even hearing the screams. She knew nothing of the accident until pediatrics called her—

the very department where she worked—and told her the child had died.

Trying to give her some peace, her husband moved her out of the Stark County house. But a few years later, on the advice of her psychiatrist, she came back and asked permission to go through the house.

"She would say, 'This is where my daughter did this.' or 'This is where she did that.'," said Joanne, who now lives in the house. "Things had been weird upstairs before, but after that it was horrible. You just couldn't go near the bottom of the steps. Now nobody goes upstairs. If you do go, you go *with* someone. There are two rooms upstairs that I desperately need, but I don't even bother. I was up there once sewing, saying to myself, 'I'm a grown woman, I own this house....' Immediately after that thought, a music box that had run down came on and played for a minute. Something strange always happens. I feel like she's up there, waiting for her mother to come back."

Joanne's daughter Anita agrees. The dead girl's room was her bedroom.

"Even though I was sixteen, I was kind of afraid to be up there. I didn't know about the little girl who had died, but I just didn't feel alone. There was electricity in the air. The lights would flicker on and off and on and off all night long. My mother thought I had an overactive imagination even though she heard things and saw flashes of light downstairs.

"There was a cloudy image in one part of the room. The cloud never moved toward me, it just hovered a little off the floor—a glowing dark greyish-white oval shape that you could see through, about four feet tall, writhing and twisting. I got the impression it was trying to communicate with me. I asked it to leave me alone. I felt a strong sense of loneliness and sadness. It was not at all frightening. But it was kind of depressing. I didn't feel threatened, only uncomfortable.

"I felt that whatever was up there would play with my toys because I sometimes found the stuffed animals in places where I hadn't left them. Looking back, I think she liked being in my

room because it was frilly and pink, and there were lots of toys.
I think she was comfortable there."

THE PIANO GHOST

Bonnie Collins of Jenera wrote me about a musical ghost
in their Hancock County home:

It had always been our dream to own a vintage home in the
country, and in the early summer of 1986, while driving in
Hancock County's Van Buren Township, I found the place. I
knew it was home as soon as I pulled into the yard—it just felt
right. We had no inkling that there was a resident spirit in our
1852 brick farmstead until Christmas, 1988. It was several
days after Christmas, and my husband had been ill. Neither of
us was sleeping well and so, when our dogs, who sleep in our
room, barked in the early hours of the morning and sat staring
at the person at the end of our bed, I assumed it was our
daughter, come downstairs to tell us that she was sick too.

I raised myself on one elbow, but froze. It was not our
daughter at the end of the bed, but a male intruder! He was
surely here to rob us, and maybe worse, I thought. I didn't—in
fact, I couldn't—move. I thought if he didn't realize I was
awake, he'd take what he wanted and leave us alone. It was
then that I realized that I could see our bathroom doorknob
through his body. This was no ordinary housebreaker!

He was an older man, slight and stooped, wearing a tan
cardigan sweater. He stood at the foot of our bed, looking at
the lowboy chest there. Then he just sort of shimmered
away....

Shortly after our first visit by the spirit we had come to
refer to as "Grampa North*"—a former owner of the house—I
was sitting on the sofa in the living room. I felt someone's wet
nose on my calf. I reached down to give the customary pat,
and found myself petting the air. The dogs were all outside in
the yard.

One night, again around Christmas, I woke in the middle
of the night to see Bruiser sitting by the door to the living

room, which was closed by a child-gate. I worried about him being there because he was an older dog and wasn't able to jump down from our bed without hurting his bad leg. When I sat up to call him, I saw he was still lying between my husband and me.

Once again, I found myself frozen for a short time, unable to move or talk, as I watched this animal, which appeared to be about the size, color and shape of Bruiser, sit looking through the gate into the living room, then turn its head and look at me over its left shoulder. Then it, too, "shimmered away."

Around Christmas, 1991, I was sitting in the living room and our daughter Jennifer was getting a snack in the kitchen. As soon as she entered the living room I knew that something was wrong.

"Who's playing the piano?" she demanded. I turned off the TV and heard the sound of one note being played on the piano, seemingly in a random rhythm. We stared at each other, all kinds of thoughts running through our heads: my husband wasn't home so he couldn't be playing, the dogs weren't tall enough to reach the keyboard, it must be a madman toying with us before he murders us!

My daughter said, "Go see who it is."

I said, "Me? Why not you? You heard it first!"

Ultimately, being the mother, I went. The only appropriate weapon I could find was my sewing shears. So, armed with sewing shears, with daughter huddled close behind, I crept toward the music room to the sound of a repeated note on the piano. I can't tell you the relief we both experienced when we found—no one! It was at that moment that all our fear over our spirit vanished and he became, to us, a friendly entity who had somehow saved us from the dreaded, imagined intruder! The piano continued for about an hour after that, then recurred several times throughout the evening.

Jennifer had bought a puppy for her boyfriend's Christmas present. On one of the nights before Christmas, the puppy cried so pitifully that my husband got up to comfort him and sat with him in a comfortable chair in the living room. It was at this time that "Grampa North" chose to repeat his concert. Having been forewarned of the musical spirit, my husband didn't panic.

The next morning, he reported to me what had happened and we compared notes. We both had determined that it was the note G sharp/A flat, two octaves below middle C, that had been played over and over.

Finally it occurred to me that there had to be a reason why almost all of the ghostly activities took place around Christmas time and why it was that just that one particular note was repeated over and over.

I had been doing research on the history of the house and its former occupants. I went to my file and looked for anything that would indicate something that had happened in the house or to the family during the Christmas season. I discovered that one of the sons of the original builder of the house had been born in the house on December 28, 1852, the same year the house was completed. I was also interested to note that the same son was married in 1875—on my birthday! But the most exciting revelation was the son's name: it was Andre Gruen*— initials A.G., the two notes surrounding the black key played on the piano.

Obviously we no longer refer to our resident spirit as "Grampa North" but as Andre. Now, whenever something happens that would have frightened us a year ago, we just attribute it to Andre and his dog.

We are very happy in our 1852 brick farmstead and very comfortable with our other-worldly residents. We feel that they add to the cozy, vintage atmosphere of the house. But we wish Andre would talk to us and tell us stories about the house and the Gruen family! Maybe, after *he* gets more comfortable with *us*....

THE GHOST IN THE MACHINE
Captured psychic images and sounds

The dead are but as pictures.
-Shakespeare-

Norah Lofts, writer of many ghostly tales, suggests that some psychic experiences are like television reception: certain people in certain circumstances are "plugged in," making contact with vision and sound already there. Dr. Margaret Murray, writing before the television age, felt that apparitions were more like photography. Light waves, she suggested, were recorded on some kind of surface, but the result would not become visible until the surface was specially treated. The development of a "negative," she said, could take a long time. And electrical storms, mist, dampness might all help "develop" a negative.

Whatever the explanation, there are many stories from people who believed they have captured ghostly images on audio or video-tape or photographs.

GRANDMOTHER KWA

R. J. Oelker of Urbana sent me this extraordinary story:

I borrowed a voice-activated tape recorder from a friend in the summer of 1992. I wanted to set it at my bedside in hopes of catching myself talking in my sleep. Having never used a recorder of this type, I decided to practice with it a little. I took it outside early in the morning so as not to be disturbed. I sat on my front porch which is surrounded by a heavy growth of trees. There were no noises except the birds chirping. After about 20 minutes, I took the recorder back inside and played it back. Beautiful bird songs came from the tiny speaker, then there was a pause, followed by the whispered words, "Bless Grandmother Kwa."

I had a little trouble understanding these words at first, so I changed the speed to "slow" and replayed the tape. At this speed, there were no words, only what sounded like a breath of air being slowly blown out. I was completely puzzled by this phenomenon. I played the tape for several friends who were just as bewildered as I was.

When my married daughter came to visit a few days later I played it for her. After hearing it, she sat in shocked silence for a moment and then told me, "Mom, Chuck [her husband] had a great-great grandmother named Kwa. She was a Cherokee Indian medicine woman. Her tribal outfit was handed down through the family and Chuck's dad has it now."

I took the tape to my daughter's in-laws' home and played it for them. They were obviously shaken. They showed me a very old picture of Grandmother Kwa which they always kept in their basement. They never displayed it because "her eyes were too spooky to look at." None of them knew Grandmother Kwa's last name.

Why I got this message, I guess I'll never know. But the story doesn't quite end there.

Everyone was so unnerved by the tape that we decided to tape over it. On playback, our conversation is heard clearly, followed by a pause and then the original message from Grandmother Kwa. It wouldn't erase!

THE FARMER IN THE BARN

Darlene Parker didn't mind things going "Hi!" in her father's Geauga County barn, but she won't go into the barn alone after a strange misty image showed up on a photograph taken there.

Mrs. Parker's father, optician Nick Halagan, his wife Pat, and Pat's father, all have heard a cheerful, clear, lilting feminine voice wishing them a good morning, saying "Hi" or "Nick."

The unusual photograph was taken two years ago at a Halloween party put on by her daughter who took pictures of a stuffed character hanging by its neck from the ceiling.

Nothing strange showed up on the photos taken with a 35mm camera but a white haze appeared on a friend's Instamatic® film.

"Before, when it was just the noises, I didn't think too much about it," Mrs. Parker said, "But after I saw the pictures, I wouldn't go up there alone."

The haze looks like very thick cigarette smoke curling in patterns near the ceiling. It stretches between two large beams about 15 feet apart. A check of the negatives showed that nothing had been spilled on them.

"It looks like smoke, but there is no smoking allowed in that barn in case of fire," said Mrs. Halagan. "We even made them put Christmas bulbs in their jack-o-lanterns."

Mrs. Halagan says the haze appears to be hovering over the hanging effigy, a chilling placement, because a man hanged himself in the barn in the 1930s after his dairy herd was destroyed for hoof and mouth disease.[1]

THE WAITING BRIDE

Dawn Marie Leigh of Warren wrote:

A few years ago I was making a video for a friend's birthday. Using a camcorder and a new tape, I recorded photos of Christmas and birthday parties that we had shared together. To introduce each party I decided to record the front of the building where the party was held. I took the camcorder to a motel in Trumbull County where we held a birthday party and shot some footage of the sign outside and the room where the party had taken place. Finally, using a new video tape, I started piecing everything together.

A few days into the project I decided to watch the tape to see how it looked so far. When I played it back I was startled to find the figure of a woman standing in front of the motel door. At first I thought it was a "ghost image" from the tape, but both tapes had been new!

For days I didn't mention it to anyone. Finally I invited a few friends to look at the tape without telling them anything about it. I was beginning to think it was just me, but they saw the figure too. And everyone I've shown it to sees the same thing.

The woman appears to be wearing an old-fashioned wedding gown. When the tape is put on "pause" and forwarded a frame at a time, it looks as though she is turning her head. The footage is only a few seconds long, but I wonder about my mysterious bride and why she is standing there. Is she waiting for someone?

THE GREEN GHOST

About 2 a.m. in May of 1990, Glynn Piper* awoke suddenly in the bedroom of his small ranch house in Twinsburg. To his amazement, he saw something that looked like a woman, hanging about a foot below the ceiling, glide from the doorway, across the room and fade out at the wall by the closet. For some ten seconds he watched the profile of a woman with straight, shoulder-length hair, wearing a button-front blouse with a Peter Pan collar. The half-length figure was transparent and was enveloped in a sickly greenish fluorescent light.

The room was dark except for the glowing figure and Glynn thought he was dreaming. He rationalized it away until a few months later when the same thing happened. This time Glynn woke his wife Elizabeth* and asked her to describe what she saw. She was more curious than frightened, but she just couldn't believe what she was seeing.

For several months the family was plagued by minor, yet spooky occurrences like lights turning on by themselves in the master bedroom and mysterious footsteps. The bedroom smelled persistently of iodine even though they repeatedly cleaned it. Their dog would not go into the bedroom when brought into the house.

Intrigued by all of this, in May of 1991, friend Greg Black* decided to set up a camcorder in the bedroom. The blinds and curtains were closed so no lights could show through. Glynn and Elizabeth slept through the taping, but at 1:14 a.m., immediately following some electrical interference on the tape, a glowing light was seen rising up from the floor by the bed, at roughly the same place the woman's apparition had appeared. The pulsating light was only visible for a few seconds, then it faded out.

A flaw in the tape? Unlikely, since the light only appears on the videotape when it is played at Glynn's house, where it was filmed. The light was not visible when the tape was played back at Greg's house no matter which VCR he tried. When he brought his VCR over to Glynn's house, the light again appeared. And nothing like the light has ever shown up on other tapes filmed with Greg's camera. Interestingly, when Greg played the tape on Glynn's TV he was able to capture the elusive image by filming the image on the TV screen. The house, which was built in the 1930s, was moved to its present site on Cannon Road in the 1940s. One of Glynn's neighbors believes that four or five members of the family who owned the house were killed when their car was hit by a train in the early 1950s. The hairstyle and blouse of the woman apparition would fit the late 1940s, early 1950s. And if she were killed suddenly, where else would her ghost go, but home?

STAIRWAY TO HEAVEN
Stairway stalkers

As I was walking up the stair,
I met a man who wasn't there.
He wasn't there again today
I wish, I wish, he'd stay away!
-Hughes Mearns-

I hear more stories about stairway ghosts than any other type of spirit. Many staircase ghosts have a death associated with them: a hanged man, a deadly fall, a murder disguised as an accident. Or it might be that the repetitive motion creates electromagnetic energy recording the imprint of a ghost upon a stair. Up and down, up and down they walk—and they never tire. Are they the footfalls of ghosts who still walk, or the footsteps of all who have trod those stairs before, echoing down through time?

THE COLD AT THE TOP OF THE STAIRS

On a bright snowy February day in 1994, Katy and I pulled up in front of a Cedarville house with turn-of-the-century trim and a wrap-around corner porch. Toni runs a little shop in the front parlor and she guided us through a room of potpourri, hand-dipped candles, and country gifts, all unusually tasteful and nicely arranged. The same flair for interior design is displayed throughout the house.

We complimented her on the house, but Toni didn't smile. She wore jeans and a sad brown jacket which did nothing for her fresh coloring. She had dark circles under her eyes.

"I just have to know if I'm going crazy," she said over and
over. I tried to reassure her that the people who call me rarely
are. Toni introduced us to her husband Dave, a mild-mannered
young man with dark hair and mustache, adding, "He doesn't
believe in this stuff."

I wandered through the shop into the front hall. The
unusually steep stairs were a rich polished brown. I stopped in
the hall at the top of the stairs. Usually heat rises up a stairwell
like a chimney, but on the landing it was freezing cold—like
walking into a refrigerator. It had been snowing all week;
obviously someone had left a window open.

"Fresh-air fiends!" I chuckled to myself.

I walked into each of the rooms off the central hall; they
were all warm and cozy. There were no windows open
anywhere on the floor. I walked back to the cold spot and
stood there soaking up the presence.

The master bedroom was colder than the other bedrooms,
but I told myself that was because it had been added onto the
house. I was drawn to a closed door. Slowly I opened it—and
nearly jumped out of my skin at the dimly wavering figure in
front of me. It was my own reflection in the glass of a gun
cabinet. But there was the same presence in the closet, trying
to tell me something urgent.

I went back downstairs and sat at the kitchen table with
Toni and her husband.

"First," I told Toni "You're not crazy. There is definitely
something here."

Then I said, "At the top of the stairs you've got one of the
most intense cold spots I've ever felt."

Toni pointed an accusing finger at her husband.

"See!" she said, her hands trembling. "See! And I didn't
tell them a single thing about this house, I swear to God. And
you said there was nothing there!"

"I didn't say there was nothing there, I said *I* couldn't feel
it," he protested.

We looked at her expectantly.

Toni took a deep breath, "A woman shot herself at the top of the stairs."

Her name was Ruth Ann. She had accidentally killed a child with her car. Unable to live with the guilt, she shot herself in her parent's house—at the head of the stair. She was only thirty-two.

Toni said, "I've heard the woman going up the stairs and dialed 911; I've seen her—she's a solid, realistic figure and she walks up and down those steps all the time. My 12-year-old daughter feels her walking in the hall. She's afraid to go upstairs by herself. She had a dream that the woman, who had short black hair, talked to her."

I suddenly realized that the woman who had shot herself had guided me to the gun cabinet. There were children—one a precocious small boy—in the house. The ghost wanted the guns out of the house.

As we talked, Toni's mother, Mrs. W.*, stopped by. Toni had told her of my visit and she wanted to know what we felt. Mrs. W. has experienced several strange things in the house, but she always denied everything to Toni.

"You have to understand," Toni's mother explained, "I know how nervous my daughter gets and I thought if we admitted there was something, she'd sit around and worry about it."

Toni admitted that her nerves have been shot by not knowing if she's really alone in the house or if the ghost would harm her. Toni seems to be an unusually sensitive woman. Living with the spirit of a suicide cannot have been easy for her, particularly when the family insists she's imagining it. "My daughter has nightmares. She's moved her bed into the corner so nothing can get her. I keep telling her that there's nothing here, but she's still terrified."

And no wonder. All this denial going on. That's what makes people crazy—not necessarily living with ghosts, but denying that anything unusual is going on.

I urged Toni to tell her daughter the truth—that the woman is there and she will not harm them.

"The ghost is as frustrated and afraid as you are," I added, "And get rid of those guns!"

On our way out I bought a painted tin night-light shaped like a little house. When you switch it on, light shines from the cut-out windows and door. As we drove away, I wondered if the cold spot would ever be warm again, or if the ghostly suicide would ever find her way to the Light that shines from Heaven's door.

THE STRANGE DEATH OF
FREDERICK ZIMMERMAN

Frederick Zimmerman stared over the fence at the rich, dark wood door of the mansion with its polished brass knocker and tall glass windows.

"Someday," he told himself, "I will lay my head under this roof."

He hobbled on. His boots were almost worn through. Back in Germany where he had been a cobbler, his friends all told him that the streets of America were paved with gold, that he could pick up silver ingots in the gutters. But New York had been a filthy, noisy place and Zimmerman began walking west. After many days, he had reached this small village— Albion in Ashland County. Seeing such a fine mansion in this small town raised his spirits. Anything was possible... Zimmerman headed into the village to look for work.

The blacksmith looked the stranger up and down. His clothes were streaked with dirt but they couldn't hide his muscular arms and broad chest. The war had taken away many of the young men and those remaining were selling their services dearly. The blacksmith could see the desperation in the man's eyes. It didn't matter that he hardly spoke any English; he needed him to work, not talk.

The blacksmith had been blessed with a family of eight girls and he didn't want to let this strapping stranger into that particular hencoop.

After the evening meal, he took Zimmerman aside. "I can't put you up at my house, but I'll tell you what—" and he gave Zimmerman directions to the very mansion he'd passed on his way into town.

"No one lives there. No one will bother you." he told the young man who looked puzzled.

"The house is empty," explained the blacksmith. "Used to belong to the richest man in town. But after his daughter—died—they moved away. No one will live there."

"Some kind of superstition," thought Zimmerman later, standing in the silent entrance hall. "People die in houses all the time; if we couldn't live in them, we'd all be out on the street—like me," he thought ruefully. And he shivered. It seemed that a wind swept down the stair's railing lying atop the carved spindles like the coils of a huge snake.

Zimmerman arranged his blanket in the front parlor and built a fire in the fireplace. Soon he was snug and warm and he drifted off to sleep.

He didn't know what woke him. Someone calling his name? Sleepily he wandered into the front hall.

Standing on the stairway landing, shimmering like a star, was the most beautiful young woman he'd ever seen. Her hair was dark and her skin pale. She wore a white dress that looked like it was woven of snow.

She glided down the stairs towards him, one slender hand laid on the stair railing. Her eyes were fixed on him and she was smiling. One tiny satin slipper crept from beneath her gown. Suddenly her smile turned to a gasp and she pitched forward, falling in a froth of petticoats. He ran forward to catch her, and was enveloped by a blinding blizzard of lace. An icy silk scarf was stuffed down his throat and he drifted into a cold sleep.

When Zimmerman didn't come to work the next morning, the blacksmith went to investigate. He banged on the knocker, then entered, his hand trembling on the knob.

He found the young man at the foot of the stairs, his neck at an impossible angle, his lips blue as if he'd frozen to death. Something was clutched in his hand. Flinching from the stiff fingers, the blacksmith slid it from the dead man's grasp. It was a piece of white satin woven with an icily delicate pattern like the etching of frost on a window.[1]

A STITCH IN TIME

Right away you know that there is something different about Dorothy Amling's 100-year-old Madison County farmhouse. For one thing, the trim is painted flamingo-pink, brighter than the flock of plastic flamingos stacked on the basketball court. For another, the house is home to a ghost.

Mrs. Amling has missed her calling as editor-in-chief of *Victoria Magazine*. The house is charmingly decorated with antiques from an old dollhouse to applique quilts. But despite Dorothy's warm welcome and the warm country Victorian decor, the house had a chilly feel to it.

"She's been restless all day," declared Dorothy, speaking about her ghost, "She's been wandering around the house."

She poured me a goblet of water. I chatted with her in the kitchen when I was struck cold by a presence at the foot of the stairs.

"She's there," I said, moving away, trying to get out of the ghost's line of sight. The presence was benign, curious, yet totally unnerving.

Dorothy introduced me to some of the other dinner guests.

"Oh, but you must go upstairs and meet the ghost," everyone insisted.

Resigned, I started up the bright pink stairs, which ran into a small landing. The right set of stairs led to the bedrooms. The left stair led into a "a strange little room off the staircase that we use for a sewing room," as Dorothy described it.

It was a cozy room decorated in Dorothy's signature colors of green and pink with green wicker furniture and a shiny green floor. And it was empty. I paced around the room while the others watched anxiously.

"She's not here," I said finally. I think everyone was a little disappointed I didn't fall into a trance and start channeling the dead woman. But the ghost peeped around the corner of the dining room as we sat at dinner and Dorothy told her story:

"We've always had things missing—or misplaced. For example, we searched madly for weeks before I found my black evening bag—hanging on the hook where it should have been to begin with."

"I bought a skirt and t-shirt set for my daughter in an unusual shade of blue. Then we couldn't find the shirt for two years. Last June she dragged me into her bedroom. There was the t-shirt lying on top of her shoes. I had gotten a pair from the closet that very morning. And I had totally cleaned the closet six months before.

"But I never saw anything until 1991. I had stayed up late for three nights, trying to get things ready for my son's graduation open house. The night before, I came upstairs at 2:30 a.m. when everyone else was in bed. I glanced into the sewing room like I always do.

"There was a lady sitting on the wicker sofa, hands folded, just looking at me. She wasn't white like a sheet, but as transparent as can be.

"I said, 'Oh, my God' and walked up the opposite stairs, and opened the door to my bedroom. 'I must be crazy,' I said to myself and I hesitated for a couple of seconds. Then I said, 'Get a grip. There *cannot* be a ghost sitting in the sewing room.' I turned around and went back to the sewing room. Nothing was there. I switched on the light. A few things lying across the sofa had been moved to the other side of the sofa. The cushion where she was sitting was completely cleared off. If I hadn't been so tired, I would have had a heart attack."

Dorothy is certain she knows who the ghost is.

"The house belonged to a woman named Minnie. Ida, her sister, spent a lot of time helping out around the house in the 1940s. A relative stopped by; Ida, an avid quilter, went up to the sewing room to get a quilt she'd been working on. As she descended the staircase, it tangled between her feet and she fell the length of the stairs. She died an hour later of her injuries."

"In our kitchen is a steel exterior door which is normally kept bolted. One night our daughter had some guests in. The boys were using the ouija board in the family room and it spelled, 'Ida.'

"'Oh, Heidi, this is the biggest joke I've ever heard,' scoffed one boy. Thirty seconds later, that locked steel door slammed open into the refrigerator, making a dent that is still visible.

"Every night we go through the house and check the doors. Several times I've woken up at 2 a.m. from a dead sleep to find a freezing cold house. Once I went down the back staircase; it was so cold it was like being in a wind storm. The wind was ripping through the house and the kitchen door was sitting wide open.

I called Dorothy in June, 1994 to see if Ida had been around recently. She told me that I was calling three years to the day from when she first saw the ghost!

"I saw her again two weeks ago. [May 1994] She was leaning against the doorway of the sewing room, more solid than I've ever seen her. I was so terrified! It was the most frightened I've ever been. I started crying. She was there for thirty seconds, maybe a minute, then she was gone.

"This past winter my husband saw her sitting in a wicker chair in our bedroom. It was a stormy, icy night. Our daughter Heidi had gone out for the evening and he was wondering when she was coming back. He looked over and saw Ida sitting on my side of the bed. He blinked, looked away, looked back and she was still there. She finally disappeared after a phone call from Heidi telling him that she was all right.

"I don't think Ida's angry, or unhappy. I think she's just here. Nothing horrible or nasty has ever happened even though when I saw her I was scared. You just feel her presence or catch a glimpse of her from the corner of your eye."

And knowing Dorothy's love for quilts and her gift for making a guest feel at home, it's no wonder Ida has chosen to stay.

THE SHY GHOST

The Circleville house was built around 1853—in the attic, you can still see the hand-hewn, pegged beams—but you would never know it to look at the spruce, updated building surrounded by flowers and shrubs. The house was converted to a double in the 1940s. Richard Patterson bought the house with his friend Susan* in 1988.

Richard's first night in the house should have been his last. He dreamed of a dark-haired young woman in a flowing purple gown floating above his bed, her arms stretched towards him, begging wordlessly for help. His own screams of terror woke the neighbors.

Ever since then Richard has heard wood creak and the tap of shoe leather as someone moves up and down the staircase, often stopping for a moment, as if someone were trying to catch a breath before continuing to climb. The night Susan moved in, he heard her on the stairway, heard doors slamming and kitchen cabinets opening. When he kidded Susan about how busy she'd been the night before, she gave him a strange look.

"I didn't spend the night here," she told him, "I locked the doors and went back to my old home."

Some nights Richard has been awakened at regular two-hour intervals by footsteps on Susan's side of the double—when Susan is at work. Susan has listened to the ghost walk up the stairs on Richard's side of the house. Sometimes they hear a low mumbled chant. Richard has heard a chorus of humming female voices. They have experienced a smell of rotting fruit in the basement stairwells which disappears as suddenly as it appears.

In 1990 Richard was sitting in a second-floor bedroom talking on the phone, facing a window that reflected the stairway landing and its light. As he talked, he caught a fuzzy image of a man in the window.

"How could anyone be looking in my second-floor window?" Richard thought. Then he realized that he was seeing the reflection of someone standing on the stair landing. He turned to look and the figure disappeared.

In April of 1993, Susan fell asleep on her sofa with her two dogs at her feet. She was awakened by her dogs growling. She heard what sounded like liquid dripping onto the stairway landing. The longer she lay there, the louder the dripping got. As the moments ticked by, she realized she had to go to the bathroom, but was too terrified to get off the sofa! Finally she was forced to get up—and found a very dry stair landing.

Shortly after that, as Richard chatted with Susan, he saw a misty, blurry white shape of a head peeking around the edge of the wall on the landing. It was almost as if the ghost was sneaking around trying to watch the two, without being seen. When it saw Richard looking at it, the head quickly darted around the edge of the wall landing and vanished.

Richard has researched the house's history. The builder was also named Richard. Patterson is the only other person named Richard who has lived in the house in over 130 years. He hasn't identified the woman in the purple gown or the person who so hesitatingly climbs the stairs in an eternal walk beyond the grave. But he did learn that a young man was killed just outside the house in the early 1970s—struck by lightning as he climbed the electrical pole to fix some wires in a storm. He was found the next day, still up the pole, with a pair of pliers fused in his rigid hands.

THE LADY DOCTORESS

First seen on an overcast day at the end of winter, the house just outside Urbana was not a promising sight: A dingy two-story carpenter gothic house surrounded by clumps of dead weeds and patches of mud down a long rutted gravel driveway. I could see the house as it had been—almost as if I had an old sepia photograph in front of me, with some somber-faced children and a woman in the wide-skirted dress of the 1860s gathered around the slab that would become the porch.

Someone stood behind the tall, pointed window on the second floor, watching. Whatever it is, I thought, It's waiting for me on the second floor.

Inside Holli led me through a knot of cats at the door. "My mom's sort of a packrat," she apologized. I noted the toy guns and tools mounted on the wall, a china-headed doll slumped inside a dusty glass bell. There was the general clutter of people who are packing to move. Holli had told me that she was buying the house from her mother and aunt and would start restoring it in June.

Holli sat in the kitchen while I prowled through the house. The main living room was empty. So was the parlor across the hall with its built-in cupboards on either side of a massive fireplace. There I opened a door to a darkened bedroom nearly filled by an antique four-poster bed. A chill swept over me. There was someone dead huddled in the rumpled sheets. I groped at the lamp by the door, clicking the switch repeatedly, only to find that it had no light bulb. I forced myself to walk across the room by the bed and turn on the bedside lamp. Of course the body was gone—there was only a smooth expanse of sheet beside the blankets, as if the sleeper had just that moment thrown back the covers and gotten up.

I retraced my steps through the parlor and into the central hall. The dramatic wooden staircase led up to a landing, then to an open balcony. The effect was of stairs flying up to an immensely high ceiling. I started up the stairs.

At the landing I stopped and pressed my back into the wall. I closed my eyes at the fear washing over me. My heart fluttered painfully. I had the impression of someone hanging from the landing railing. The feeling passed as I started up the stairs again. In the room to the right the ceiling was badly water-damaged. There was a smell of mold, but the room was empty.

Through the small attic door I could see daylight under the eaves, a general clutter. I moved on to the next room; the room to the left of the landing. There the flowered wallpaper was covered with graffiti, giving the effect of a tattooed skin. Shelves flanked the tiny window. Figures of horses, a music box, and other trinkets were tied to the shelves by cobwebs.

The room looked like it had been abandoned in the fifties. Misery, I thought. In this room, I felt, someone had been very unhappy. I went out and closed the door.

I looked over the stairwell at the gothic window. I had saved this for last. The window was set in a niche and I had to stoop under the projecting part of the slanted ceiling to get to it. As I stood up again in the alcove, I felt a light spidery touch on my hair, as if someone were running a tentative finger along it. I looked up to see if I had caught a hair on the beam, which was a good foot above my head. I shrugged.

The glass of the gothic window was wavy. I looked down the lawn to the road. Someone had stood there, watching for one who never returned. I shook my head. I was getting a very strange feeling of gender confusion—a man disguised as a woman or a woman passing as a man; or possibly just a masculine woman or feminine man. It was all very odd.

Back downstairs Holli and I sat down in the living room.

"The landing of the stairs..." I began. Holli buried her face in her hands.

"The stairway is where the ghost walks most often," she told me.

When I mentioned the dead person in the bed, she panicked.

"But that's my mother's bedroom!" she exclaimed.

I reassured her that this was an *historic* dead person—a long-dead dead person, and not a vision of the future.

I told Holli about the touch on my hair and the gender confusion I had felt in the alcove. "I don't understand it," I confessed.

As Holli sat with her back to the hall and I faced it, I suddenly felt the ghostly woman standing on the stairs. "She's there," I said quietly to Holli.

"I know, I can feel her," she said just as quietly. The woman was tall and had strongly beautiful features. Her dark hair, parted in the middle was drawn back at the neck. She wore a white work dress c. 1910 with the sleeves rolled up.

The son of the previous owners, who only stayed in the house six months, gave this same description when he was a child: a lady in a white dress on the stairs, her hair in a net, and her sleeves rolled up. He saw her float, glowing, into his room, then she floated back out the door. Holli used to dream of a woman in white floating up and down the stairs.

She and her brother lived in the house until 1988.

"My brother and I would lie in bed waiting for something to walk in the door. To this day my brother will not discuss the house or what he experienced there."

"When I was dating my husband, there were only certain times my mother would allow him to spend the night at the house. One night we pretended to say goodbye and then he sneaked back upstairs. Later I went downstairs to the bathroom. When I came back, he said that somebody had walked in the room and hit him on the soles of his feet with a ruler!"

As we talked, I wandered into the hall, glanced into the parlor, and blinked. The room was full of smoke. "Ah," I thought, "it's the silvery wood paneling causing that smoky effect." Then I turned and saw smoke drifting by the mirror in the hall.

"It's just the paneling, right?" I asked Holli hopefully. She didn't know what I was talking about I was getting something about a stove overheating. When I explained, Holli told me that the parlor stove caught on fire around 1910, burning out the front of the room.

As if saving the best till last, Holli showed me a yellow and black sign painted, "Mrs. Dupler, Female Physician" and on the reverse, "Mrs. S. Dupler, Doctress." The sign had been found, sealed up in a wall by the upstairs alcove when Holli was eight.

Holli had worked hard to uncover the secret of "Mrs. Dupler." The woman's father had been a doctor. She was widowed the day after Christmas in 1868. She married a man named Rhodes who died in 1888. Dr. Dupler herself died in 1912 in Plain City. She is not buried by either of her husbands.

Doctoress. Female Physician: A strong-looking woman in a masculine profession. Not buried by either of her husbands....

I went away fascinated by the story. About two weeks later, I returned with Anne, Katy and my daughter. I had told them nothing except the house was near Urbana. They went through the house while I sat in the car. Anne saw the front parlor as the "doctress's" office, while the back bedroom (with the dead person) had been an infirmary. Anne and Katy also strongly sensed the fire in the parlor. And Anne "saw" the same sepia photograph of the front of the house as I had.

The lady physician took a kindly interest in my daughter. We were sitting on the sofa when my daughter murmured, "She's sitting next to me." and shrank shyly closer to my side.

Katy also felt very strongly that the woman wanted Holli to find something, that Holli would find it as she restored the house. Holli has almost been obsessed with the idea.

"We found a pigeon's blood glass vase under the floor in the right bedroom. And a shoe. And the sign. I'm ready to dig up the basement, only I'm afraid of what I might stir up!"

On my second visit I met Holli's mother who has heard the lady rustling up and down the stairs.

"One night," she told me, "when the kids were young, I was out bowling. I had been a bad girl and stayed out later than I should. As I was walking up the stairs to check on the kids, I felt a hand slap me on the bottom as if to say, 'You stayed out too late!'

She laughed, "I don't bother them; they don't bother me!"

Holli is now preparing to move into the house and bracing herself for the major mess, and expense it will take to make the house beautiful again. She is not so obsessed with finding out the house's secrets. She knows they will be revealed in good time. And she is sure the lady doctoress is on her side.

"As I was stripping wallpaper in the one bedroom, I almost heard her say, 'Much better! You're putting it back the way it was.'"

I MET A MAN UPON THE STAIR

From the road the house outside Springfield looked tiny—a doll's house with fresh white paint and shiny green trim. But the back revealed additions many times in many generations. Katy and I commented on the original outhouse and spotted the foundation of a summer kitchen beneath the snow-crusted grass.

Jennifer, a rosy blonde with a calm air, her tall and lovely dark-haired daughter Niya, a dog and several cats came out into the crisp air to welcome us. By the back door I noticed steps going down into what looked like a crypt. Jennifer laughed and explained that the "crypt" was actually the original springhouse.

We walked through a narrow kitchen with a frieze of antique potholders of many different colors and shapes, an old tin milk box, a basket of muffins on the stove. A warm love for the past filled the house. An antique refrigerator stood on the polished wood floor of the dining room near a 1940s coke machine, a cupboard displaying cheerful 1920s kitchen accessories, and a mission oak desk. Just inside the living room, a glass-fronted cabinet housed Native American flints and stone tools. Jennifer's husband, Donald, is Shawnee.

Despite the many antique touches, the house seems almost as sparsely furnished as it would have been in the 1840s when the house was built. Maybe it was the shining wooden floors. Or the plain plaster walls. Or a time warp...

After we discussed a little of the history of the house, I explained how I like to inspect a house. Jennifer retreated to the kitchen. Katy went off in the direction of the dining room and I stepped onto the stair landing through a small door cut in the wall. It seemed rather cramped, but the original house had ended there.

I looked up the stairs, shuddering, and immediately felt the blood draining from my face. I hesitated. Niya was still standing in the living room. I didn't want to frighten her but I wondered if she had ever felt the horror crouched, leering at the top of the stairs.

The thing stepped aside as I pushed my way to the top, past a wall of books, and around the stairs to son Thurin's room. Old-fashioned built-in wood cupboards made the small room even smaller. The presence grew stronger. I was chilled to the bone, but I was also determined to find out what was causing my terror. I sank down on the bed, clutching my notebook to my chest.

"If you have something to say," I thought, "I'm listening." I watched a small closet door in an alcove, and waited for something to come out of it.

"I'm cold," a voice entered my head, "I'm cold...."

From the window beside the closet I could see a tiny window shaded with green mini blinds. A secret room?

Katy stood in the doorway.

"It's male," she said. I was going to remind her not to talk about the ghost until we were done, but my teeth were clenched and I could only nod.

Then the presence eased and I went into Niya's room. It too was tiny. There was a dressing table, silver comb and brush set, antique metal bedstead, stuffed animals, figurines and photos, a cluttered alcove of a closet—all the normal teenage trappings. But I also seemed to see the room as it had been: stark and bare, with one low bedstead. How do they stand this? I wondered.

At the top of the stairs I noticed the titles of the books in the bookcase. *Koko, The Dark Tower, Advanced D&D*, rows of notebooks labeled *"Heavy Metal"* with some kind of monster on the spine.

"These aren't helping matters," I remarked to Katy. She looked, started, and shook her head.

She had already been in the attic, but I twisted the wood toggle and opened the small door under the eaves.

"You don't want to go in there," she warned, but I had already ducked my head inside. Then I pulled back.

"There's a smell?" I said tentatively. Katy nodded. "Formaldehyde and—what?"

Once more I bent to the door—and shuddered. Suddenly something rushed at me from inside the attic; my head snapped back with the violent impact. I jumped out and slammed the door, my back braced against it.

"My God," I said, "my God..."

Katy nodded wisely. "I told you."

Shaking, I went back downstairs, thinking, "How in the world am I going to tell them about this?"

Jennifer and Niya seemed serenely unaware of the thing in the attic. I didn't want to scare them, but the presence was not a healthy influence.

"It's male and he's angry," Katy said flatly. "He's very religious, very fundamentalist and he's angry about the books in the hall."

I knew that the books were one focus of the thing's anger. I had thought it was just because an interest in D&D and horror books often stirs up negative ghostly activity.

"Did they have hired hands on this farm?" I asked Jennifer. I was getting a picture of a farm worker who slept in the far corner of the attic by the little window. A man of Scandinavian descent.

Katy got a much clearer picture—a man in his 40s, but worn out before his time by hard work. Sharp features and a big jaw. Not very bright, and obsessed with his religion. We agreed that he dated from the 1920s or 30s.

"It must be awful for him," I told Jennifer, "thinking he was going to go to Heaven and here he is stuck in some crummy attic. For him it's still 1930."

Sitting in the living room I could look at the ghost more objectively and pity him. Lost spirits can feel like they have bad intentions since they have such strong, almost negative energies. The ghost was angry and I am terrified of angry people.

Jennifer and Niya were sympathetic. "I feel sorry for him," said Jennifer, "We'll do what we can to move him on."

She explained about the attic. "We all take buddies into the attic. I'm *quiet* there. But my husband gets very angry when he has to go in there. He bangs around and swears, and gets violently angry."

I later interviewed Donald by phone.

"I never really feel comfortable up there," he admitted, "I seem to get upset about the mess and end up swearing. I feel like I have to go clean things up because nobody else will. Everybody just sticks stuff inside the door and shuts it.

"Before you came, Jen wanted me to straighten out the attic. I was up there with no one home, grumbling to myself, 'I can't believe the kids can't put this stuff further back. I'll put it all back in that corner.' Instead, I cleaned out the corner. Everything was out of the way or pushed away from that far window. I really went to a lot of trouble to neaten that area up!

"I'm a little afraid to go in there. Spirits should go on. I stuck poison for the mice up there. I didn't even go in. I just pitched it."

Thurin, too, admitted, "I never liked the attic. It was creepy. I was putting blinds up in there and I didn't want to finish. I was getting really paranoid. I told my Mom, 'You can ground me if you want to, but I can't go back in there.'"

The ghost also hides things. Niya told of putting some makeup samples in the bathroom. "I looked there four times and then later found them right where I'd looked."

Thurin had his driver's license papers in an envelope in the drawer in the dining room desk. The day he went to take his test, they weren't there.

"I guess we're going to have to get a whole new set," Jennifer told her son. He looked once more, and there were the papers: right on top.

Jennifer told of waking to see a small boy wearing a brown vest and knicker suit, standing right in front of her, studying her curiously. Perhaps, we speculated, he came from another era and told his mama about the strange ghostly woman in the parlor.

Everyone in the family has seen a mysterious black pup with floppy ears. A few days before we visited, Donald heard whining and rustling and saw a little black dog in the dining room.

He thought it was their dog Makwa, but then he saw Makwa on Niya's lap. When he looked back at the dining room, there was nothing there.

Jennifer told us how, when she was taking a load of laundry upstairs, she found a dog tag in the middle of the stairs.

"I looked up, thinking it had falling through a crack in the ceiling or something."

She showed us the circular brass tag stamped, "Aurora Dog License, 163 1929." If any records remain, perhaps they would show the license belonged to a little black dog...

When I spoke to Jennifer in June, 1994 she told me she had seen the little boy again, in roughly the same place, only this time he seemed about a year older. Jennifer also said the children are not afraid of the attic anymore. "I'm still a little nervous. I don't want to push it. But I realize he's mellowed," she said of the farmhand's ghost. "I think he's accepted us and the fact that we're all here together."

4

LANTERNS FOR THE DEAD
Ghostly lights

I'm not afraid of the dark, I'm afraid of what's in the dark.
-Anonymous-

"Go to the Light."—That is what spirit rescuers tell earthbound spirits who cannot find their way. Yet, paradoxically, it is ghost-lights we fear.

Ghost lights have long been part of ghostly lore. From the will-o-the wisp luring unsuspecting travellers to their doom among the marshes to the corpse - candles flickering among newly made graves, spook-lights have haunted the imagination for as long as men have feared the dark.

THE LUMINOUS TOMBSTONE

In Dayton's historic Woodland Cemetery, there is rumored to be a tombstone that glows in the dark. One autumn evening in 1994, I was filming a TV show at Woodland with my ghost-hunter friend, Anne Oscard. I finished my segment, then wandered off in the dark to wait for her interview to be done.

I wasn't thinking of glowing tombstones or really of anything in particular. I certainly wasn't afraid since I enjoy graveyards. But suddenly—directly in front of me—loomed a luminous tombstone.

It was about six feet tall, shaped like a narrow Gothic church window with a pointed arch at the top. It glowed warmly, like light bulbs behind translucent glass. It was a soft white light, not the faint, greenish glow of mosses that grow on old tombs.

My heart started pounding. I simply couldn't believe what

I was seeing. "This time," I thought "I've lost it for sure…"

I stood there in the dark, gazing at this incredible stone glowing in the darkness, my breath getting shorter and shorter. Then I steeled myself to walk forward, to take a closer look.

The closer I walked, the brighter the stone looked. Then its shape began to change, to dissolve into something less definite. My mind could hardly comprehend what was happening. Then the picture clicked into focus.

And I found that my glowing tombstone was only the lights of the bars on Brown Street, darkly outlined by the arching branches of two ancient trees.

MY GRANDFATHER'S STORY

I was fooled by an optical illusion, but I doubt that this story, which my grandfather who had the family sensitivity to seeing spirits, always told with relish, had so simple an explanation.

It was about 1910. He and his brother Johnny were roaming around the land where the Galion Golf Course now stands. They were digging for something [just what he never said] and they were up to their eyebrows in the hole when they saw a lantern bobbing across the field.

"Johnny kind of squinted at it and neither of us could make out who it was that was carrying the lantern. Well, we both scrunched down in that hole and waited for the man or whoever he was to walk past. And he did, but when he was close enough for us to see who he was, there wasn't nobody there! It was just a light bobbing along by itself. Johnny got so scared he got up out of that ditch and ran the three miles home."

CORPSE CANDLE

Bernard of Belpre sent me this story:

"My two brothers and I were born in Marietta on Pike Street. We lived through many high waters and the depression years. Our mother always told us we were so poor we didn't even know when the depression happened.

My Mother and Dad finally had all the floods they could stand and managed to buy a house that had been burned out on

St. Mary Avenue. They rebuilt the inside and we moved into it just days before the 1937 flood came.

We did not notice anything strange on St. Marys Avenue until all three of us boys were in our teens—in the late thirties, early forties. I was the youngest. There was a street light in front of our house and this is where all the kids came to play. We almost always were outside till ten or eleven o'clock.

We were out as usual and it had started sprinkling rain, but it took more than a little rain to make us go inside. As we were looking up the street toward the Catholic Cemetery that is located at the end of St. Mary's Avenue we saw a light start moving from there like a lantern and it moved steadily all the way up on top of the wooded hill and around the ridge where the waterworks now stands. The amazing thing about it was that it never swung or moved up or down but moved in a steady line like there were no trees or ruts to cause it to falter.

We did not get real excited about this until once again on another night, I don't know how long after the first time, it happened again. We were a little braver then and we said, "Let's find out what it is." So we ran into the houses and grabbed a flashlight and started running as fast as we could toward the light. It was hard going through the woods and I figured our lights were going in all directions, but the light we were chasing continued on a steady level journey. At last we were coming within fifty or seventy-five yards of the light and it vanished as mysteriously as it appeared.

THE BLUE LIGHT GHOST

In the 1930s a girl named Anna* lived in Sugar Grove. She was engaged to marry Fred Lee*, but folks in Sugar Grove wondered if they'd either of them live to see their wedding day, the way they fought. They'd scream bloody murder at each other, then kiss and make up and the kissing seemed to make up for the fighting.

But one day they had one fight too many. They kissed and made up as usual, but people said Anna was never quite the same afterwards. She was subdued, numbed somehow. Yet there was a gleam in her eye that made people shudder to see it.

One night as Anna and her lover sat parked on a covered bridge, she pulled out the knife she'd hidden in her bag and cut her fiance's throat as dispassionately as if he'd been a hog that she was butchering. Then she hacked off his head, sawing through the tendons, disjointing the backbone until the head came free, as easy to heft as a melon.

Anna carried it up a nearby hill. There she sat down, cradling her lover's head in her lap. Murmuring an endearment—he was hers now and forever—she cut her own throat. The coroner said she had risen and walked steadily a little ways down the hill, to judge by the trail of blood. She was clutching her lover's head by the hair when they found her.

To this day Anna's ghost still walks down the hill. It is best seen on a moonless night or a night when there is no full moon. If you get out of your car and call "Anna!" into the darkness, you will see a glow, a bluish haze around the top of the hill. Then it will congeal into a vaguely human form and move down towards you, a luminous column, not flowing as we imagine a ghost to move, but stepping like a normal person would, on her way somewhere.

But where is Anna going, striding down that hill, as if she had somewhere to go—besides Hell?[1]

THE LOST GHOST

Some psychic researchers believe that ghosts are stirred up by house renovations. Frozen in time, the dead still see the house as it was when they lived there. Often they are pathetically confused.

On a sunny, late-spring day, Rosi and I visited Janet's house in a small Warren County hamlet. It was small and upright like its owner—a no-nonsense, humorous, plain-spoken former journalist. Rosi and I liked her at once.

I was taken with Janet's antiques and memorabilia, but the house also held a subtle disharmony not easy to identify. Janet had filled the home with many plants, lots of light. Yet it was haunted.

Rosi and I prowled through the house, taking notes. Something was wrong with the staircase. Something was wrong with the whole floor plan upstairs. Rooms flowed into each another at odd angles. What the Chinese call the *feng shui* of the house had been disrupted.

I found the ghost in the upstairs hall. It was a man and he was upset and confused. I didn't blame him. The strange angles were getting to me too. I opened a door into a storage room, the only room that looked as if it hadn't been altered. The presence was strong there.

"What have you done to the upstairs?" I asked Janet.

"We closed up some doors and added two from the hall." Janet said, "We removed some walls and took out the front staircase."

"There's your problem!" I said, "Your ghost is still seeing the house as it was when he was still alive. He's confused—trapped—caught like a bumblebee in a bottle. Show him the way out."

Janet told me, "After we remodeled the house and changed the steps, we would hear the kids go to the bathroom or come down the steps, but we wouldn't hear them go back to bed. My husband began to tease me about having a ghost."

The first time Janet left the children home alone, they met her at the door, David holding a sword cane.

"Are you just coming home?" he demanded "We thought we heard you coming upstairs."

"'Mother, someone's knocking on my door,' my daughter would complain. 'Mother, someone's turned my doorknob.' We had an intensive week or two until she stripped the hall wallpaper and repainted."

Janet believed the ghost was an early owner. I wasn't so sure that she wanted the ghost to leave. It almost seemed to be company for her. And he was helpful. There was a tricky water heater in the basement. Dangerous, but something Janet had been putting off fixing. One day she found the switch had been turned off. She got the message and put in a new heater.

After lunch, the three of us pulled up in the driveway behind Janet's house. Rosi and I walked around the side of the car. Simultaneously we looked up at the half-curtained upstairs windows. We could see the upstairs ceiling.

"You know, I get the feeling he's watching us," I murmured to Rosi.

"You took the words right out of my mouth," she laughed. We took two steps. A huge tree temporarily blocked our view of the house. Beyond the tree, we looked up again. A ceiling light was on in the back bedroom.

"Rosi," I said tensely. "That light wasn't on just a second ago, was it?"

"I was just going to ask you the same thing."

Janet smiled as she unlocked the back door. "Sometimes he does that, just to say, 'Hello, welcome back!'"

5

CAUTION! GHOSTS AT WORK
Ghosts in the Workplace

Work, for the night is coming....
-Annie Coghill-

SUFFER THE LITTLE CHILDREN

For generations, the rich and elite of Dayton sent their retarded, handicapped, and illegitimate children to a farm on what is now Research Park Boulevard. It was not a place acknowledged or spoken of. A place where the keepers—as if the children were animals—doled out food and medical attention grudgingly. Some children were beaten and mistreated by the guards. And if a child suddenly sickened and died, no one asked too many questions. The farm grounds were littered with small graves.

Now a research organization, stands on the site—a citadel-like building of cement and steel-blue tile, mottled with rain the day I visited.

"I've seen ghosts in the building," Lesly told me. She worked as a cleaner there in 1989.

"The first time I was over there," Lesly told me, "I got images of children playing tag, running from place to place. They were transparent and they came within a foot of me. I could see a hand reaching to touch me.

"'No, I don't have time for this,' I said, 'Go on and play somewhere else. I can't play right now.' And they ran off and I saw them off in the distance playing....

"Once I saw a chair move, as if somebody flopped down in the chair and crossed its legs and said, 'What's going on here?'

My sister saw a child with Down's Syndrome at the escalators, only ten or fifteen feet away.

'Oh, what do you want?' she asked him. He just looked at her. She turned around, then turned right back. He was gone.

"As I looked down a hallway, I saw what looked like a male figure—a blurry face, a body silhouette of a big man with his arms crossed. I felt he was giving me a really mean look, a hard stare. While the other figures were light, this figure was dark. Something about his presence gave me the willies!

"A security guard who works at night has seen and heard a male and female ghost having an argument. She told them to shut up, she was listening to the radio. They did, and went away.

"For a whole week before Halloween in 1990, I heard doors opening. I'd check. Nobody there. Closer to Halloween, somebody was whistling a tune. I couldn't tell what the tune was, but it was like someone trying to remember a song or trying it out. I told my supervisor. He said that I was hearing things."

One night when Lesly heard the whistling, she asked a man working late if he heard it. He had. He went and checked the next office while Lesly worked on. Nobody was there.

"Halloween night I went in late because I had to hand out candy at home. I heard furniture moving. There was whistling, on and off. The closer it got to midnight, the noisier it got. I hurried up and got gone! And there were no more noises or whistling November 1."

The baby farm was taken over by Children's Services in the 1950s. Cruel guards, beatings, and midnight burials became a thing of the past. In 1980 the farm was closed and torn down.

The curved driveway just in front of the building is outlined with stout cement pillars. One of these pillars, originally lifted into place with a crane, kept repeatedly popping out of the ground. Lesly wonders if some of the children are trying to push out of their graves.

They would have to be very strong to lift the pillar. But perhaps they don't need to be strong—just patient. And they've got forever...

A GHOST YOU CAN COUNT ON

Built in the opulent pre-Depression era, when banks were designed to impress customers with their wealth and stability, the eighth floor at Cleveland's Federal Reserve Bank boasts carved black walnut paneling, life-size oil portraits of former financiers, and painted ceilings dripping with wrought-iron chandeliers. The walnut tables in the conference rooms do not levitate; the dead financiers do not step out of their frames to warn of a coming stock plunge. But Fed employees, as well as security guards and cleaning women in the nine-floor granite building have seen a ghost they call Matilda Rose Brennan.

Those employees were ordered not to talk about Matilda. Banks, after all, deal in real, solid things like coins and contracts. To have an intangible asset like a ghost floating around the place would shake up the most hardened securities officer.

"Yes, we have an employee who believes she saw a ghost," Federal Reserve spokeswoman June Gates was quoted as saying in the August 14, 1992 *Plain Dealer*. "But we consider it a rumor and don't want to comment on a rumor."

The executive whose office is cleaned by one of the woman who witnessed the spirit says he was told Matilda is in her twenties with long, curly, light brown hair, dressed in a 1920s dress—the time when the building was built. Although he did not see the ghost, he has been teased by his fellow executives: "Are you carrying a rosary? Are you going to perform an exorcism?"

Why Matilda Rose Brennan? Some say the name was plucked from the ether by a pair of psychics brought in to find the ghost. Another employee says *she* named the ghost after doing some research on the building's history; she did not elaborate. Since the ghost wears 1920s clothing perhaps she was a victim of the 1927 stock market crash.

Matilda hasn't touched anything, just glides around the halls and offices. "It just appeared and didn't cause any problems. I mean, we're not talking about the Amityville Horror here," said the Fed spokesperson.

They say you can't take it with you. But it could be that the Federal Reserve ghost is trying.[1]

IN THE HALL OF THE MOUNTAIN GHOST

Rogue's Hollow used to be known as the toughest damn spot in the United States. Five miles south of Doylestown, it was a rough coal mining town full of saloons and gambling dens. The land beneath was honeycombed with mine shafts. It was said that you could easily walk the seven miles from Clinton to Hometown underground.

Rogue's Hollow was home to many spooks, including Peg Leg Pete, the one-legged wagon driver; the headless horse who haunted the ghost oak; and giant snakes. (See the "Buckeye Bigfoots" chapter in *Haunted Ohio II*.) Even the mines were haunted.

It had been storming all day, but Frank Herwick, a saloon keeper, who dug coal on the side, ignored the distant rumble of thunder as he shoveled coal into a car. It was heavy work and he paused for a moment to wipe the sweat out of his eyes.

Suddenly the dimness of the mine was turned into blazing day. Lightning zipped along the iron rails into the gallery where he was working, writhing in snakey rivulets along the floor. Then he saw the ghost.

The glowing white blob was just standing there then it glided forward from the coal face. Suddenly all of his picks and shovels began to dance. The picks rocked madly on their curved heads like demented rocking chairs. The shovels wobbled and spun. The mine car swayed back and forth while the coal was juggled by invisible hands.

The ghost glided back and forth, watching. Another lightning bolt sizzled down the tracks and there was a thunderous explosion as if the mountain were coming down. Herwick did the only sensible thing: he ran. And he never went back. He was happy to turn the lease of the mine over to someone who didn't believe in ghosts.

Today, the mines of Rogue's Hollow are abandoned by all but the shadowy figures of ghostly miners still on the job.[2]

DEAD MEN DON'T WEAR PLAID

In 1966 Renea Hodge was a stockroom clerk at the JC Penney store in Columbus' Great Southern Shopping Center.

"It was early morning, about 7:30 a.m. I was there with Charlie*, a guy who also worked in the stockroom. The Assistant Manager, Karen*, had let us in; we were the only people in the store.

"Karen asked Charlie to replace some burned-out bulbs. They both went out front while I stayed in the stockroom and got the machine ready to price some merchandise. About ten minutes later I heard someone walk into the furnace room next door. I thought Charlie had come back and I started talking away to him. No answer.

I yelled, 'Well be that way! Don't answer me! See if I care!'

"About that time he came up behind me and said, 'How's it going?' and walked on.

'Wait! How'd you do that?' I said.

'What?'

'How'd you sneak around to this other side from the furnace room? Somebody came in here and walked into the furnace room and hasn't come out.'

'I haven't been in the furnace room. Well, I guess you heard our ghost.'

Renea was skeptical. "Oh really? Well, whoever, it was, they weren't very polite, they didn't answer me. No, you really were over in the furnace room, weren't you?"

"No, I've been changing bulbs."

"That's when he told me Karen was scared to death of the place. She wouldn't even go inside by herself, but would sit in her car and wait until someone else got there.

"Karen had seen the guy—and the woman. I guess we had two of them. The female ghost was tall, thin, very properly dressed in late 40s style with high heels. You could hear her heels click across the floor.

"Karen was in her office when she saw *him* go by. He was a light-skinned black man in a dark grey suit with a Clark Gable mustache—like Billy Dee Williams. Karen thought he was the manager of the men's department. She went out into the hall, followed his footsteps, and found nobody in the dead-end hall.

"She flew downstairs, where she ran into the *real* men's department manager. It just scared her to death!

"As for me, my daddy always used to say, 'You didn't do anything to them [the dead]. They know who did, they just want justice. If you didn't hurt them, you don't have anything to worry about.'

Renea heard when they were building the building, workers had dug into a couple of unmarked graves. Would a thirst for vengeance explain the two smartly dressed phantoms strolling through the store? Or perhaps they just want to update their post-mortem wardrobe.

TO HELL AND BACK

The massive old iron furnace stands like some sacrificial stone tower at Lake Hope State Park. In its heyday the furnace blazed like an altar to Baal, turning out ingots by the thousands. Towns and railroads sprang up to serve the furnaces and their workers.

The furnaces were guarded day and night. One night watchman liked to walk the narrow ledge of the furnace chimney, looking down into the inferno with the comfortable assurance of one who is no immediate danger of going there.

One stormy night as the guard walked along the rim swinging his lantern, he was struck by lightning. He was dead long before his charred corpse tumbled into the white hot molten iron.

Today the towns are gone; the furnaces are cold. But hikers caught in thunderstorms sometimes see a lantern and an outline of a man walking the rim of the furnace—a man who's been to Hell and back.

MOTEL HELL

Vivian Flint of Columbus sent me this intriguing story:

In the Fall of 1981 I was living in West Virginia and going to school in Ohio. I would attend computer classes for a week, then work for a week. This arrangement had been going on for over six months and frankly I was tired of it. This four and a half day class at the IBM Center in Cincinnati would be my last course.

My secretary always made hotel arrangements and even though I got written confirmations, I would always call and confirm my reservations. Unfortunately things were so hectic before this final trip that it completely slipped my mind. I think there must be a Murphy's Law about this, because when I got to the Cincinnati hotel on Fountain Square, there was absolutely nothing available, not so much as a closet!

After much arguing and a few threats on my part, the clerk suddenly said she had a room for me. She said they usually didn't rent it out; complaints about the heating ducts, I recall her saying. She stressed that accepting the room was completely my decision. Grateful for a place to stay after my long drive, I took it.

The room was at the end of a short corridor in a part of the hotel I never knew existed. I was puzzled by the desk clerk's insistence that the hotel was completely full because this section was deserted. I also couldn't see any trace of the ductwork the other occupants had supposedly complained about. I decided the clerk didn't know what she was talking about and congratulated myself on getting a room with a lovely view of the Cincinnati skyline.

I had my usual busy day, but a few things were odd: I had a lot of trouble falling asleep. Although I like my room dark, I couldn't bring myself to close the drapes. Usually I'm in bed by 11 p.m. during the work week, but this time I would read until 3 a.m. every night before dropping into an exhausted sleep. I simply did not feel comfortable in that room.

Each morning at 7 a.m. I would be awakened by the sound of a man using the bathroom. As a married woman I was familiar with the noise and passed it off as poor insulation between the rooms. I remember thinking it was strange, though, that I was privy to that noise when the only other sound that ever filtered into my room was the occasional sound of a distant door shutting.

In the wee hours of the third morning, shortly after falling asleep, I was startled awake by the sight of a man standing beside my bed. He was silhouetted against the window and my first thought was that he was a burglar. But he was staring so intently at me, my next thought was of rape.

Fighting to wake up, I sensed an overwhelming feeling of extreme hatred and malevolence radiating from the figure. As I watched in astonishment, the man before me lost definition and slowly faded away. I then realized that I was sitting bolt upright in bed, heart pounding wildly, staring at the dawn sky.

I finished my course that morning. It took all the self-discipline I had to make myself go back into that room to pack. I checked out without mentioning anything to the hotel staff. I just wanted out!

I memorized the room number, just in case the hotel tried to foist the room on me again. Over the years I have forgotten it, but I have not forgotten the experience—and I know one thing—it was no dream.

WORKED TO DEATH

Lori, an assistant in the Registrar's office at Columbus' Franklin University, was the type of worker who was truly faithful unto death. Although she was a midget and suffered painfully from scoliosis, she was always cheerful and efficient, becoming a good friend and advisor to Angela Granata when Angela joined the staff.

Lori died suddenly in 1984 when she was just twenty-five. After her death, no one could find five student transcripts she had been updating. On Saturday, Brian, who also worked with Lori, asked Angela to help him find these vital files. They searched the office, through all the drawers and files they could find. But they couldn't find the files.

Brian knew that he would have to recreate the files on Monday—something that would take days. But Security wanted them out of the building so Brian and Angela had to give up. Half-joking, Angela told Brian, "You know, I'll bet Lori will be back to take care of this mess since she never left a job unfinished." Then they left, and the building was locked up for the weekend.

On Monday Brian called Angela and thanked her for finding the student transcripts.

"What are you talking about? I don't have a key. I haven't been here since Saturday."

Brian was bewildered. He called all the other staff members. None of them had been in the building. Security said no one had come in Sunday. Obviously Lori had delayed her departure so she could come back to finish the job.

THE PHANTOM WOODMAN

It was a Thursday night, summer, 1993 at Camp Beaumont. Hank, an Assistant Scoutmaster, and his friend Mike decided to go off by themselves. They hiked about three miles down the Beaumont trail and then headed off the trail. They found the perfect campsite: a large field with absolutely no other campers. Everyone else was on the other side of the reservation.

It started to get dark. They got a fire going, toasted their hot dogs, baked some apples, then decided to build the fire higher for the night. They collected wood, more than enough, they thought, and settled in for the night.

Hank and Mike talked for about three hours by the fire, then noticed the unusual cold. They also noticed that their fire wood was nearly gone. Should they head into the woods for more? Lots of rattlesnakes in the area, they agreed. And decided to pass on foraging in the dark.

The young men climbed into their sleeping bags. Hank was just putting his head on his pillow when he heard something walking in the woods.

"Mike and I both sat up in our sleeping bags at the same time and peered into the woods. We could not see anything, but it seemed like the person would walk for a while, stop for a few seconds, then start walking again; all the while getting closer. After about two minutes, we saw someone come out into the clearing with his arms outstretched, holding something. It was a man wearing a red flannel shirt and old blue jeans. He was carrying big pieces of wood and the moment I saw that, the hair stood up on the back of my neck.

According to camp legend, a long time ago a man was camping in the Camp Beaumont area of Ashtabula County. The day had been warm, but that night the temperature dropped drastically. He hadn't collected enough wood for his fire but was afraid to go into the forest after dark for more because of the bears. He tried to make his wood last, but was found frozen to death several days later. Now he appears at campsites running low on wood.

"The man steadily walked towards us, and when he got about five feet away from the fire pit, he carefully put the wood down. He then looked me straight in the eye and smiled a smile so friendly I thought I was looking at my mother. Then he turned around and went back into the woods. We heard the same pattern of footsteps and he re-emerged with another armful of wood. Again he carefully put the wood down with the previous pile. He looked at us and smiled that warm, friendly smile, but did not say a word. He walked into the woods, where we heard him for about five seconds, then there was complete silence.

"That pile of wood lasted us till exactly sunrise the next morning.

"Mike and I never told anyone this until now. That night

was the coldest night in summer camp history. I can't be sure, but I think that ghost woodman saved our lives."

LONG OVERDUE

It was whispered that the original Ashtabula Library was built on a Native American burial ground. Actually it was a pioneer cemetery, although all the bodies were supposedly removed before the library was built. But what wanders the basement hallways and second floor is neither an Indian nor a pioneer, according to Pat, who worked at the library until 1989.

"Ethel McDowell was named librarian when the building was first built in 1903. She was a spinster cliche of a librarian—steel-gray curls, steely *grande dame* posture—and she ruled the place with an iron hand!

"In 1968, Miss McDowell retired. She died shortly afterwards—then came back to make sure things were being run right. Her portrait hung in the library and it wouldn't surprise me if she came out of her frame and walked around!"

Miss McDowell's special domain was the reference room on the second floor. When the area was later used for storage (mostly for books of Miss McDowell's era) there were often stories about mysterious footsteps. And books that didn't fit Miss McDowell's high standards would simply disappear. "Ethel didn't like that one," joked the staff, who found old books lying open in the middle of the floor.

In October 1991, just before a major renovation was finished, a fire destroyed the whole thing. Fire fighters poured water through the roof for six hours. Authorities never came up with an explanation for what caused it.

"The rumor among the staff was that Miss McDowell did it because nobody discussed the renovation with her," said Pat.

The architects' drawing of the new building had been displayed in the library for months before the remodeling started. On the facade was a carving of a lion taken from the 1903 building. As the staff was moving the drawing out after the fire, someone took a second look at it: The lion's face looked eerily like a death's head.

"But I did it from photographs," protested the bewildered architect.

"We told him to get his colors out and fix it NOW. Had we just not noticed it? Or had unseen hands edited it?"

The ghost was often glimpsed in the basement hallway. Patrons and staff always swore they had just seen someone go around the corner, someone who looked like Miss McDowell, although no one ever got a clear view. There were also intermittent cold spots in that hallway and people thought they heard voices when they were there alone.

Pat, who ran the Children's Department said, "Things flew across the room. The children swore they didn't do it, but I can't make any promises. There were always weird things with the lights, heat, and fuses.

"It might have been me," Pat laughed, "I didn't exactly run a ladylike children's department—a department that Miss McDowell would have approved of. I let them play *Dungeons and Dragons* in one corner. It was pretty noisy; if the kids kept it under earthquake level, I let them get away with it.

"In those days the library wasn't automated: books were checked out by removing a card from a pocket in the back of the book. One day, half of the day's circulation just disappeared. *Two years later,* I found that day's circulation cards sitting on a table in the children's section. They weren't sitting on that table for two years. I'm not an organized person, but I would have noticed that!

"My assistant Sandra* did storytimes. Once when the theme was farm stories, I suggested *Hatty and the Fox.* But during the storytime, I noticed Sandra wasn't reading that book. Afterwards she asked me if I had taken it. She had put it on the table beside her, the children came in, she reached for it, but *Hatty and the Fox* was gone. Sandra hadn't stirred from the chair and the book hasn't been seen since.

"I don't know why," Pat laughed, "Unless Miss McDowell liked it so much she had to have her own copy of it! It *is* a noisy story. I've never quite come up with an explanation for that one."

The renovations have been completed now and the library is quieter, although many lights still blow out and doors stick mysteriously. Nobody is quite sure if Miss McDowell, an Institution in her day, still hangs around the institution. Said Pat, "She was so much a part of the building for so many years." Perhaps she still is.

HAUNTED HINCKLEY

Most people associate the town of Hinckley with buzzards. The dirty birds return there every March 15th like rather ungainly clockwork, possibly commemorating the carnage of the Great Hinckley Varmit Hunt of 1818. But when I think of Hinckley, I think of an 1840s white clapboard house, quintessentially New England in spirit, that houses the Hinckley Library.

Today it is a cozy place, well-lit and well-stocked. But back in 1973 the structure was condemned as unsafe. It was then that Friends of the Hinckley Library had a vision that the house would be the ideal place for a library. Elaine Vanderschrier worked with the group to buy and restore the building.

Stopping at a traffic light by the library one warm evening, Vanderschrier had another sort of vision.

"I happened to glance in at a library window in the hallway and noticed a light was burning. I could see a young woman sitting on the stairs. She wore a blue dress and had her elbows on her knees and her chin in her hands."

Vanderschrier didn't think much about it at the time since workers often stayed late. "The traffic light changed and I turned my attention elsewhere, thinking perhaps someone was working on a project." She half-noted the woman's high neckline and very old-fashioned hairstyle. "But during the next few days as I was checking schedules, I realized that no one should have been there...."

A few years later, a staff member from Brunswick glanced into the same hallway and noticed a man in a hat peering at her through the bars of the stairway. She paid little attention, then realized he was acting strangely. She went upstairs, but found no one there.

"Now you must remember," Vanderschrier said, "that this building is an old home with one room opening into another. It is not a place where people can wander around and not be seen.

"When our computer system was being installed a staff member from Medina who had some experience with the supernatural came to Hinckley. When we told her our stories she decided to see what she could unravel."

What she found was this:

Dr. Nelson Wilcox, who lived in a log cabin on the property, was one of the pioneer school teachers of the area. He was regarded locally as "a walking encyclopedia." According to local historian Judge A.R. Webber, this learned gentleman wore a "plug hat at all times, whether in his garden or on the streets."

His photo shows a figure with a patriarchal beard like John Brown and a mass of hair like a thunderhead above his brow. He has deepset, piercing eyes and an uncompromising slit of a mouth.

The pensive young woman in the blue dress might be Wilcox's sister Rebecca, who died tragically young. She was, according to Judge Webber, "handsome in form and feature and beautiful in character, artistic in her taste and skilled with her needle. Anything that came from her hand in the dress line was regarded as the best. Her untimely death in youth was mourned by the entire township for "none knew her but to love her."

The Medina woman also found Rebecca's grave. Although she had never been to the cemetery before, she walked right to a toppled tombstone and said, "this is it"....and it was. Her epitaph reads: "We miss thee at home."

Several years ago Vanderschrier found a pair of delicate, antique embroidery scissors while weeding a flower bed.

"Probably there is no connection to Rebecca," says Vanderschrier, "But it is a tantalizing premise."

The staff member from Medina claimed that the spirits took on their forms very deliberately. Rebecca was a seamstress so Vanderschreier noticed the blue dress. Dr. Wilcox always wore a hat, so that was what the Brunswick staff member noticed.

This all happened several years ago and there have been some sporadic recent sightings. Says Elaine, "Books on ghosts, hauntings, and ESP still fall off shelves; maybe that's from the big trucks rumbling by. But since Dr. Wilcox was called 'a walking encyclopedia' we assume he's happy with a library on his old homestead."[3]

GELEERD'S GHOST

It was a tall, narrow, rather lonely-looking building. The street level was painted brown with a rich yellow ochre trim. The top two stories were of a fine-textured cream brick with two elegant bay windows. Above the top window, the date "1899" and a curly initial *G* were picked out in red paint. Six little lion's heads peered down at me from the cornice. This was the setting for the story Rick VanLandingham III told me:

My mother had a frame shop and art gallery in downtown Toledo. One day she glanced up at a building on Adams Street she walked by daily. She saw the beautiful bay windows and the date "1899" carved in the stone cornice and immediately fell in love with the building. My mechanical engineer dad realized that while the building was structurally sound, it needed tons of cosmetic work. But he knew better than to try to discourage my mother. At one point he said to her, trying to call her bluff, 'It's me or this building.' She didn't hesitate: 'The building!' she said.

The summer of 1985, I spent a month cleaning garbage out of the building. You have to understand that the previous owner, Kevin*, was an alcoholic and into some very questionable activities. Although he ran a wholesale pet supply store it was rumored that he fenced stolen property.

Kevin had been involved in an unsavory affair that went

bad. Someone whacked him on the back of the head with an ax and he bled to death in the basement. His body wasn't found for several weeks—what was left of it after the rats had been at it. There was still a blood stain on the floor.

The basement had been used as a dump. We found everything from exploded cans of pet food to dead pets. It was like a little pet graveyard down there. A rat had climbed into the main breaker box and had been electrocuted. The fried skeleton was still hanging out of the box.

I researched the whole history of the building. The building must have been beautiful when it was built. Once you know the history, it brings a house alive. For me it came alive in more ways than one....

Built by the Geleerd family in the 1880s-90s, it had housed a cigar manufacturer, billiard hall and cigar shop, boarding house, and, on the third floor, the Geleerd residence. The father died while it was being built; Mrs. Geleerd kept the family together and the sons helped run the business. She lived on the third floor for the rest of her life and died there.

The third floor was the most interesting. As you came up the long narrow stairway, you immediately felt like you were moving into a different world, a different time, a place where you could still breathe 19th-century air. In one room you could stand at the window and imagine looking out onto street 100 years ago. That room, more than any other, could transport you back.

The floor was practically untouched since it was built. The private entrance for the original owners was never bricked up, they just slid a bookshelf into the space. It was exciting to be the first person to step into that opening since it was filled in— like a doorway to the past.

I had strange feelings in the rest of the building. But on the third floor there was a tingly feeling, like you get when lightning strikes too close. At night when it was pitch black, it was a scary place! If I had to go fetch some tool my dad had left up there, I'd feel this sensation at my back. But I'd be darned if I was going to run down the stairs for something that wasn't there! I didn't say a word to anyone. I didn't want anyone thinking I was crazy or overly imaginative.

We were nearly done with the first and second floors, but the third floor still needed a good cleaning. I worked all day. When Mom came by that evening, I wanted to show her how nice and clean it was. We walked up the stairs with our flashlights. As my Mom and I were talking on the landing, I suddenly had a strong feeling like someone was behind me, about to tap me on the shoulder. Immediately I turned and ran down the stairs. About the second floor I said to myself, what are you doing? You just left your Mom up there and you've got the flashlight! So I went back up.

"Are you OK?" she asked. She could see how nervous I was. I blurted out, "I don't know about you, but I felt something!" and I told her that I had felt a person walking right up to us ready to say something. I felt really silly. She said it was OK, but I wasn't convinced until she explained.

I never expected my Mom to be a psychic kind of person. But when she first toured the building she had a strong impression of a woman about her own age or a little older. The presence told her "You will buy my building and fix it up and make it right again, not like *he* did."

My Mom didn't see anyone, but could describe the person—Eastern European features, on the heavy side, wearing wire-rim glasses, silvery hair in a bun, a dark dress with lace around the neck and a brooch. I thought it was an awful lot of detail for someone she didn't see! But the presence had been quite firm about it: it was her building, she was its guardian.

After that I'd test the feeling. I'd bring a group of friends or Mom's clients who hadn't been told anything and take them on a tour. Each person, even straight-laced business types would remark on a "strange feeling." Some would ask if there were some loose wires because it felt like electricity. Others would say straight out, "There's a presence here."

In my sophomore year of high school, an elderly lady introduced herself. She was taking care of a very elderly lady, the granddaughter of the original owner. The granddaughter had spent a lot of time in the building as a child and we invited her to visit. She turned out to be very much a Victorian-era woman with a beautiful way of speaking. She could barely walk so Mom sat her on an antique chair about as old as she was. She showed us a photo of her grandmother.

When I saw that picture every hair on my neck stood up. I turned white. I had to sit down. I was sure I was looking at a picture of the presence. The photo matched my mom's description exactly. Mom wasn't shocked; it was as if she had expected it.

I believe that some, if not all, of the presence was bound up with the fabric of the building—the energy of lath and plaster and woodwork affected by the energy of the people who lived there. The place meant so much to me—I left some of my own energy there. The building is owned by a group of lawyers now; they appreciate it. But I haven't been back since. It's too hard to let go.

Mrs. Geleerd, too, found it so.

THE HAUNTED TRUNK
And other ghost-infested objects

And the crack in the teacup opens
a lane to the land of the dead.
-W.H. Auden -

Does furniture possess a soul? Can a house be haunted by the ghost of a rocking chair? Here you will meet some truly inhuman spirits: A possessed sheet. A trunk that contained more than clothes. A haunted typewriter. Then look over your shoulder as the clock strikes thirteen....

THE HAUNTED TRUNK

Around 1971 Judy and her husband Jim purchased an old immigrant trunk from an antique dealer in Pleasant Hill, Ohio. It was held together with iron strap hinges, had a domed lid made of three individual boards, and it was big enough to hide a man. It dated from 1720-40 and was painted with faded red buttermilk paint.

When the family moved to an 1854 brick house in Champaign County, they cleaned up the trunk and put it in the family room. Immediately Judy found herself inexplicably terrified of certain rooms at night, certain that an intruder was in the house.

Judy's mother, who is blind, came for a visit and complained of Judy walking around all night, up and down the hall and stairs. Then when Judy returned from an errand, she found her mother with her back pressed up against the door. As a joke she touched her mother's arm and said, "Boo!"

"My mother jumped straight up. She had felt a presence going up the stairs. She said to it, 'In the name of the Father, Son, and Holy Spirit, get thee hence!' The menacing presence forced her back down the stairs."

Jim's sister also asked why Jim kept going up and down the steps all night. She saw a very tall dark-bearded man in old-fashioned clothes. Young daughter Beth saw him too. To the children he seemed very solid, very real and very mean! When Beth saw him striding down the hall towards her she ran to the bathroom, crawled behind the toilet and screamed.

After Jim's sister refused to visit any more, Judy called in the neighborhood "white witch." The woman brought in a silver needle suspended from a tripod which she placed on different pieces of furniture. It didn't react to anything until she put it on the trunk. The needle quivered, then went in a circle.

The woman asked questions and the needle moved one way for yes, another direction for no. According to the oracle, there were two people associated with the trunk: a man and a girl. The girl had brought the trunk from Scotland when she eloped with her lover. Her father followed the couple, killed his daughter, and then himself. His violent spirit couldn't rest.

Judy asked the antique dealers if they knew any history of the trunk. The answer came back swiftly: An ancestor of the original owners had brought the trunk from Scotland, they said. And, according to family legend, she had been murdered.

Jim was skeptical. He moved the trunk to the foot of Brian's bed. Then Brian said that he saw the menacing tall man at night, that the man picked him up.

Finally, since she couldn't stand to destroy the trunk, Judy sold it to a friend who laughed at the idea of ghosts. The friend died shortly afterwards and when her husband sold the trunk, Judy lost track of it. So if you find a coffin-size trunk, painted a faded red, at a bargain price, let the buyer beware—you might be buying a murderer.

THE FISH IN THE MIRROR

In 1984 Nancy Small bought an older house in the Dennison West area of Columbus, on a dead-end street near the Scioto River. Built around 1900, the house needed a lot of renovation so Nancy put her three teenaged sons to work. The first thing they noticed in the empty house was the large number of religious statues and wall plaques. Made of brightly painted plaster, they stood on the floors and the mantelpieces and hung on the walls. None of the Smalls could remember seeing them when they inspected the house. The boys moved them from room to room as they worked and finally stored them in the basement.

Nancy's boys worked very hard, sanding, painting, and papering. Everything looked so nice that Nancy took photos of all the rooms. When she got the pictures back, she was startled to see the smoky outline of the Christian fish symbol apparently inside the flattened oval mantel mirror.

"Oh look," she told her family, "There's a ghost. They always show themselves in photos and mirrors." They all laughed at Nancy, but she went back and took another roll of film. The fish showed up in the mirror again, this time swimming in the opposite direction. The family didn't laugh.

Several years later Nancy decided to sell the house. Her real estate agent had once lived next to the property and one day he told Nancy, "I heard that 'Mad Mary' died."

"Mad Mary?"

"That's the nickname the neighbors gave to the woman who sold you your house."

Nancy filed this bit of information away and forgot it. The following summer she went to a service at a Spiritualist church in Columbus. Out of the blue the service leader paused at her pew and said, "Mary is trying to get hold of you."

Spooked, Nancy never went back to the Church.

A CABINET OF CURIOSITIES

Michael Berger, formerly an Educational Coordinator at the Cincinnati Art Museum, told me these stories from the Museum:

In 1985, Jim,* a security guard at the Cincinnati Museum of Art, was strolling through the upstairs painting galleries late one weekend afternoon. Off the Spanish Renaissance painting gallery is another gallery built to resemble a church apse of about 500 A.D. with wall paintings on the rough stone walls and dome.

Casually Jim glanced into the church gallery. There in the doorway was a black-draped figure. It was nearly seven feet tall, draped in an inky-black hooded robe with long, full sleeves. He stared for a few seconds, then his mouth fell open as the thing rose into the air and went through the ceiling.

A couple of years later, he still gasped for breath as he told about it. He swears it was the most terrifying thing he'd ever seen.

There are other eerie spots in the museum. A dark bronze cast of a tomb sculpture for Frank Duveneck's wife, Elizabeth, is known jocularly by some Museum staff as "The Dead Duveneck." It lies in eerie state in a gallery by itself and some guards have seen a ghostly female figure rise from it and hover over the sculpture.

Many Museum treasures are seen only rarely because of space limitations. In the depths of the Museum was a storage room holding a number of pieces of oriental furniture, carved in dark wood with strange, twisted figures, some with inlaid eyes of mother-of-pearl that glittered in the dim light. Two maintenance workers were in the habit of slipping into this room for after-lunch naps. Frank* had just stretched himself out on a roll of Turkish carpet when a noise made him open his eyes.

There, suspended in the air, only a few inches from his face, was a glowing, greenish, demonic face. The face grinned at him. Frank yelped and scrambled to his feet. He dodged around pieces of furniture, but wherever he went, the demon's face blocked his way, leering. Somehow he got out of the room and fled to the locker room in search of his buddy Ted*. He tried to act nonchalant, but Ted looked at him strangely.

"You don't look so good. You saw it too, didn't you?" Ted asked. And he described the same ghastly green face.

When Frank told this story he wondered if the thing came out of some piece of furniture stored in the room. After all, he said, look at those carvings of demons and monsters and dragons that writhe over Chinese furniture. The sculptor had to use something for a model, didn't he?

MIRROR, MIRROR

Mirror, mirror on the wall—are the dead really on call? According to Dr. Raymond Moody, author of *Reunions: Visionary Encounters with Departed Loved Ones,* anyone can use the technique of "mirror gazing" to see the dead. He cites some startling success stories. Long before Moody, the ancient Greeks used the "psychomanteum," a room with a mirror in which to contact the beloved dead. And on a cold, windy night in late 1918 a group of women stood on the corner of Rose and Main Streets in Chillicothe, exchanging comments about their recent experiences with a "magic mirror."

One had seen a woman, holding a baby. Another saw a good-looking man who waved at her. The youngest woman, almost in tears, refused to tell what she had seen.

It had all started when the Fitzgerald* family noticed something strange while eating dinner: if they looked into the dining room mirror, they could see strange scenes and figures on the plain plaster wall reflected in the mirror. Unbelieving, the family asked a few friends to sit at the table, look into the mirror, and tell what they saw. Each saw something different.

News of the eerie reflections spread quickly throughout Chillicothe. People flocked to the home and begged for a look.

One by one they were allowed to sit at the dining room table in the flickering gas lights and gaze into the mirror.

The visitors saw many different visions. Almost all agreed the scenes appeared in shades of black and white and gray. Sometimes they seemed to swirl in a fog; sometimes they were crystal clear. One woman saw a man wearing a crown. Another saw a little child in a robe of grey mist. A man saw the head of a beautiful horse, with arched neck and flowing mane. Some people saw only the wall behind them. Others went away ashen-faced and would not tell of their grim visions. The Great War was raging in Europe and for many people, anxious for loved ones in the service, the pictures brought only horror.

The strange pictures attracted so much attention that the police asked the Fitzgeralds to stop admitting visitors. The mirror was finally removed to the attic. And that was the end of the magic mirror of Chillicothe.

If it hasn't been broken, the mirror may still exist in some dusty corner. If you own an antique mirror, you might want to hang it across from a blank wall, sit down, and watch what unfolds. But first ask yourself: do you really want to know?[1]

THE WATCHMAN

Do the dead know what time it is? In 1893 a county employee noticed that the clock in the Butler County Treasurer's Office had stopped. Later, as a watchman patrolled the building shortly after midnight, the clock in the Treasurer's office began to strike. It struck twelve—and went on striking. As the curious watchman stepped to the door, the stroke became painfully loud and seemed to shrill with an almost-human tongue. The clock struck twenty-one times and fell silent.

Then the watchman saw a shadowy human face superimposed on the clock face. It was a desperately sad face, the face of a man tortured by a secret, but unable to speak. The watchman believed he recognized the face of a previous watchman who had hung himself in the vault of the Treasurer's office in the 1860s.

But according to the *Middletown Signal,* the alleged suicide was murder. The watchman slept in the Treasurer's office to guard the money kept there. Four government officials who had embezzled large sums plotted murder. The watchman was the only man who could discover their theft and dead men tell no tales....

As the watchman slept, the men pumped ether into the vault until the watchman passed into a deeper sleep. Then they hoisted his body to the chandelier and let him hang, an apparent suicide. Investigators noted the tell-tale odor of ether, but no one was ever arrested or prosecuted for the murder. Two of the alleged murderers were still associated with county government in 1893, according to the *Signal.*

Do the dead know what time it is? Perhaps it was to haunt his unpunished murderers, that the watchman's ghost still counted the hours at the courthouse.[2]

A FACE OF CRUMPLED LINEN

Carmela told me of her experience in a house off Sylvania Avenue in Toledo in 1958:

Mary and I were both twelve at the time. Her mother had died only two or three weeks before and I was spending the night at her house.

As we lay in bed, with a battery-operated lantern for a night light, the door to her room opened just a crack, not enough for a person to get through. We could see the light in the hallway.

Then a sheet slithered in the door. It grew taller, then shorter, weaving around like a snake. It draped itself over a chest of drawers and changed shape and size. At times there was a bulge on one end, like a head; a moment later it would be sharp. The only thing the sheet never did was rise completely off the floor.

We screamed! Mary's Dad called to us to shut up—from downstairs. So we screamed for Mary's teenage sister Janet to stop it! "What are you talking about?" demanded Janet from her room next door. But she wouldn't leave her room to see what we were screaming about.

Mary threw the lantern at the undulating sheet and missed. Next she grabbed a bottle of nail polish and threw it. The lid came off, the sheet splattered with polish and —bang!—that sheet fell down flat on the floor. Mary kicked it into the hall and slammed the door!**

BONE OF MY BONE

When Eddie* was a boy, he and his Uncle Joe were great buddies. Uncle Joe would take Eddie and his friends to go off-track betting, and Joe always went to his nephew's baseball games. But when Eddie was 15, Uncle Joe got cancer and moved in with Eddie's close-knit family. Two years later, he died.

"When he died, that's when the weird stuff started happening," Eddie remembers. "Like my bed just all of a sudden used to shake. The whole bottom half of the bed would just start vibrating. Nothing else in the room would move."

Eddie believes that was Uncle Joe's way of telling him to straighten up. "Ever since I've calmed down and gotten married, those things don't happen," he claims, "But I also think Uncle Joe followed me to Tiffin."

This time the specter left his mark.

When Eddie and his wife moved to Tiffin, Eddie brought along Uncle Joe's razor and kept it in an upstairs bathroom. In the middle of night, the water in that bathroom came on full-force. As Eddie stumbled through the hall, he wondered if Uncle Joe was hanging around again. The next morning he knew.

**Will the lady from the White Oak Inn who told me this story please contact me at the address on the order blank.

There, in the upper left corner of the bathroom mirror was the skeletal print of a man's right hand. The imprint showed every detail, even the joints of the boney fingers.

The mirror goes all the way to the ceiling of the bathroom. "For anyone to have put their hand there, they would have had to climbed onto the counter." Eddie's wife Paula* said. She wiped off the image, only to have it reappear—three times. Then it was gone.

"I went out and bought a crucifix and it hangs next to my bed," says Eddie, a hint of nerves seeping into his laughter, "I figure Uncle Joe must have followed me."[3]

QWERTY

In 1984, in her Toledo home, Glenna set her electric typewriter on her grandmother's old farm table and began to type a school test. She had worked only a short time when the typewriter jammed. Puzzled, she poked at the keyboard. It was completely locked up. She turned the typewriter off, then on again. It was still locked.

Tinkering with it, she pushed each letter in turn. Suddenly it let loose at O, then jammed again. In the second row, the letter L printed, then it jammed again. She stopped, afraid to go any further. Her late grandmother's name had been Viola, but everyone called her Ola.

The next morning her skeptical husband tried the keys. They all worked.

"I felt like it was my grandmother making her presence known. Just a couple of weeks later I stopped at a red light. As it turned green, I felt a hand on my shoulder and turned around. There was no one there. Before I could turn back and accelerate a car came whizzing through the light. If I hadn't felt the hand and turned, it would have crashed into me."

MEN IN BLACK
And other ghostly gentlemen

*It was the man in black...who was the deadly one, the kind of
man you knew at a glance you couldn't touch and live.*
-Fritz Leiber-

THE MAN IN BLACK

One summer evening in 1974 Rick Hamm was cruising
across the Viaduct Bridge in his '64 Chevy heading for Twenty
Mile Stand. "I got almost to the end of the bridge and I saw this
real tall black man. Everything about him was dark. He was
about six foot eight, sharply dressed in a solid black mock
turtleneck and black suit, and his head was shaved. He was just
leaning back on the railing, half-sitting, half-standing. He
looked like a normal guy, except he was so tall!

"My headlights were shining directly on him. He started
smiling at me. When he looked at me, his eyes turned white
and started beaming this silver light. I didn't want to stop. I
knew it wasn't anything normal."

Yet Rick pulled into the Comet Gas station just down the
road and turned around.

"I've got to see this thing again," he said to himself.

In place of the man in black hung a cloud of white smoke.

There was no place to park a car nearby. Rick saw no one
else around. It was a hundred-foot drop to the shallow water
underneath the bridge. There was nowhere the man in black
could have gone.

Hamm thought that was the end of the story. But in 1978
he was sitting in the HR Block office in Springdale looking

through *Cincinnati Magazine* when he found an article, "The Men in Black." It told how a man had been fixing dinner when he suddenly felt someone outside. He pulled back the curtains to find a tall black man pressed up to the glass. His eyes started beaming white light and he disappeared into white smoke.

"I've been there," Hamm thought.

He called up a former classmate who lectures on UFOs and other occult subjects and told her what he had seen. "What do you think of it? Who are they? What are they?"

The woman speculated that the man's silver eyes meant purity or goodness. "He wasn't going to hurt you," she told Hamm, "When he beamed at you, he was communicating some kind of information."

"Then why don't I *know*?" Hamm asked me in frustration. "I believe there's go to be something to all of it; there are enough strange sightings from reputable people like pilots. And I always think to myself, is this the night I'm going to see him again?"

THE DOCTOR IS IN

Bob* lived on Jackson Street in Dayton's Oregon Historical District for about eight months, sharing the 1870s house with two roommates—and one ghost.

The ghost was a tall thin man, always impeccably dressed in a black dress suit and a top hat. Bob saw the man quite frequently—twenty times or so. The last time, the ghost actually tapped him on the shoulder.

I believe that if a ghost in a black suit and a top hat tapped me on the shoulder, I'd think the undertaker had come for me, but Bob is an engineer and made of sterner stuff. When Bob's landlord heard about it, he suggested that the spirit was a Dr. Idling, the man who built the house. Doctors dressed very formally in those days, upholding their professional dignity. Or the ghost might have been one of the doctor's unluckier patients. It turned out that Bob's bedroom had been Dr. Idling's examination room.

Bob was quite skeptical at first. His roommates were a different matter. The first time Mark* walked in the door he knew the house was haunted, feeling a strong presence. The third roommate refused to enter Bob's room after dark.

No wonder—after what happened to Bob. One night Bob awoke suddenly with a sense of something looming over him. He rolled over, thinking that Mark was playing a joke. It seemed to him that Mark was up over the bed on a ladder holding something behind his back that he was about to throw at Bob.

Bob said sleepily, "Mark, that's not funny, go back to bed."

Then he looked again. The thing wasn't Mark and it wasn't on a ladder. It was floating above the bed and it was holding something that looked horribly like a tombstone. The creature raised the stone above its head as if it was about to hurl it onto his bed. Bob gasped, and before he could find out if the tombstone truly had his name on it, the ghost vanished.[1]

TALL, DARK, AND HAUNTED

In the mid-1980s, WJW TV-8 Cleveland studio camera-man Art Lofredo, went up to the third floor to check a schedule.

"I ran into Shirley, one of the cleaners. She was trembling and her eyes were the size of half dollars. With a quiver in her voice, she told me that someone was standing at the end of the hall, someone tall, all black—just standing there, not moving or speaking a word."

While Art peered down the hall towards the back storage area Shirley said, "You'd better go back there and check. Someone might be wandering around the building who doesn't belong here."

"I don't see how anyone could get past security," said Art "but I'll go check."

Hesitantly he walked down the hall and checked the storage area, bracing himself for the moment that someone tall, dressed all in black would leap out at him. He looked behind boxes and doors. Nothing.

Even though he tried to reassure Shirley, she was still trembling and upset. She went back to her work looking over her shoulder.

Several days later Art saw Shirley again. She seemed even more upset. "I saw the same tall, dark figure at the end of the hall. When I turned and saw him again he immediately disappeared!" She insisted it was the same figure, just standing there quietly looking at her.

In spite of his own fears, Art again went down the hall to the storage room and spent fifteen minutes searching among the piles of boxes and props, through all the nooks and crannies. Again nothing.

Shirley left the station in 1988. In 1992, Art was talking with a security guard on the second shift. Somehow the subject of ghosts came up and the guard mentioned that a newly-hired guard had seen something strange in the first-floor hallway. He'd passed the hall and glanced down it to see a tall, dark figure dressed all in black standing there. He kept on walking, then did a double take and backed up. The hall was empty.

For the first time, Art told his friend about the tall man in black Shirley had seen; how he'd searched the area and found nothing. The new guard quit as soon as he heard the story; and, after that, Art's friend refused to patrol the third floor.

DYING BY INCHES

Bev wrote:

We moved into the house in Cuyahoga County in 1962 when I was four. Almost immediately the "crashes" started; several times a week it sounded like an entire shelf of pots and pans had collapsed in the laundry room. My Mom or Dad would rush there, only to find nothing out of place.

When I was about five years old, I woke up in the middle of the night and was just lying there thinking about how my Mom always told me there was a guardian angel over my bed to watch over me. I felt pretty safe. Until I looked into the hall and saw "the Man." It looked to me like the hall or bathroom light was on (my Mom says it wasn't) and he was standing about twelve feet from the foot of my bed, his feet apart, his arms hanging loose. "Daddy?" I thought. "Coming to check up on me?" Then I noticed the figure was pitch black, just like a black silhouette. Suddenly, he moved. He didn't walk, he just moved forward about six inches. I blinked. He moved again! I was in absolute terror! Then he moved again, about six more inches.

I realized he was coming into my room and there was no way I could get around him. I closed my eyes tight and lay there, frozen with fear. I felt him walk up beside my bed. Then after what seemed to be about 20 minutes, I opened my eyes a little at a time and he was gone.

The next morning as soon as I heard my parents' voices downstairs I rushed to tell them what I'd seen. My Mom pooh-poohed it, saying, "You had a dream." By the time I was eight years old, I knew the house was haunted, but I kept it to myself. I started hearing "the walking." Shuffle, shuffle, shuffle, out of the laundry room into the kitchen and then the living room where it would make quiet stirring noises like it was looking for something.

Eventually my parents swapped rooms with me. One night, my sister, who was about four, was sleeping between our parents. She rolled over and there at the foot of my parent's bed was a solid black man. She knew it wasn't Daddy because she was right between him and Mom. She squeezed her eyes shut and didn't open them until daylight. When she told my mother, my mom got a funny look on her face. I jumped up and down saying, "I told you! I told you about that a long time ago!" I was glad my sister saw it. It made me not look so crazy.

Sometimes when my sister and I were home alone, we would hear someone get up out of our parents' bed, which had a squeaky spring, open and close the closet door. One Christmas I was home from school sick when I heard the bed squeak, the closet door open, and felt someone looking at me from the hall. I ran downstairs and stood—terrified—in the front door between the storm door and the entry door for almost two hours, waiting for my mom to come home from work.

Occasionally I also heard "the talking" in the attic over my bedroom: several women, babies, and children enjoying themselves. I stood on my bed trying to hear what was being said, but I never could understand them. They were enjoying themselves, like at a baby shower or a Tupperware® party.

On a beautiful sunny Saturday morning when I was seventeen, I was home alone, shaving my legs and primping for a date that night. The last thing on my mind was a spook. Suddenly, just outside the bathroom door I heard heavy huffing and breathing, like a man who has been running very fast or someone who is extremely angry. I shut off the water and listened. It was definitely a man.

"How did he get in?" I wondered, "Maybe it's Daddy and something's wrong."

"Daddy!" I called. No answer, just the breathing.

I started to panic. I couldn't just lock myself in the bathroom. Nobody was expected home for at least an hour. Finally I threw my razor around the doorframe. Instantly the breathing stopped. As soon as it did, I ran, shorty p.j.s, shaving cream, and all to the front door. When my Mother came home she said the noise was the water pipes. (Five years later, she heard the same breathing in the same spot.)

After I was married, my Mother told me that she had heard "the walking" as well as "the talking" but they couldn't afford to move and she didn't want to scare me. [!!] My parents still live there. I think that they think if they don't talk about it much, maybe nothing will happen. My Mom will not take a shower without someone in the house. She has a watchdog who also hears "the crashes," and she will not go in the attic alone.

My Mom will swear that "the man" is gone. That's the only way she can stand to stay there.

JAMES

When the first flat black cutouts of men leaning up against trees began to appear in the Miami Valley, they gave me the willies. I've heard too many stories about ghosts that look exactly like these cutouts—ghosts that were like flat black shadows that walked. Like James.

Robert* and Carol's* houseghost first manifested himself in January of 1991 in their 1960s ranch in Waynesville.

"I'd been in the hospital with surgery," Carol told me. "I was sitting in the family room on the end of the house and I asked Robert to get the scissors from the kitchen counter. The counter was piled high with mail and stuff."

Robert took everything everything off the counter top then reported that he couldn't find the scissors. So Carol went out to look. The scissors were not in the kitchen or the bathroom. But when she returned to the kitchen, the blue-handled scissors were lying in the middle of the snow-white linoleum floor.

Carol lay back down and pondered this. Then she heard someone going through the papers on the countertop. She called to Robert who didn't answer. Miffed, she called him again, more sharply. He answered her from the bathroom. He scoffed when Carol said, "Robert, we've got a ghost!"

Feeling a little foolish, Carol began talking to the ghost. "I told him, 'If you want to stay, fine; if you want to go on, fine, but you're not going to make me leave.' That's when the ceiling fan came to a dead stop, like someone was holding onto the blade."

Robert and Carol call the ghost "James" after the man who built the house and who died in their son Daniel's* bedroom.

"My son's door slams a lot. One day Robert was playing chase and hid in Daniel's room. The door slammed shut, then opened just a crack. I saw Daniel pushing on the door, but it would not open, although it was still cracked."

Carol yelled, "James, leave the door alone!" At that, the door slammed open and bounced off the wall.

James also likes to aggravate Carol by interfering with the laundry.

"I'll put a load of laundry in and shut the lid. I'll go upstairs and when I come back, the lid will be standing open half an inch. I shut it again. In another half hour the lid will be open again. It sometimes takes me three or four hours to do the laundry."

James plays with the stereo. "You can sit there and literally watch the button being pushed in and then the stereo goes on. It can't be a short, when I watch the button going in and out! And personally I do not go into the bathroom after midnight until daylight. The toilet flushes with me sitting on it and it's scary!"

Finally James showed himself.

"He was just a flat black shadow. I put him at about six foot three inches. Weight? I don't know how to judge the weight on a shadow. A friend of ours who knew James said he was six three or four. That's enough evidence for me. He's almost like a shadow on a wall, yet he has more of a three-dimensional form, almost like someone standing there dressed completely in black.

"One night, I fell asleep about midnight with the TV on. The remote had fallen between the bed and the wall and the timer was not set. My husband woke up at 3:30 a.m. and found the TV off.

"The next day my daughter Alyson* asked, 'Mommy, who was the black man who turned the TV off last night? He was standing at the foot of the bed. He looked at you; you were asleep. Then he went into the kitchen. I followed him. He went to the dining room and the living room. Then he disappeared back in the hallway by my room. I got scared and went back to bed.'"

Robert wants to see him. He says, "I feel he looks out for us; that he's a protecting spirit. But sometimes he spooks me. He'll raise and lower the lights in the dining room, using the dimmer switch. If I'm trying to read or write, it makes me sick. But all I have to say is, 'OK, James, that's enough.' I feel like I'm being watched all the time, like he's standing or sitting beside me."

"Robert had a talk with him when I was gone," Carol recalled, "He went into the living room and lit some candles and talked to the ghost, asking 'yes' or 'no' questions. He said to James, 'If you want to show yourself, fine. But we don't want you to show yourself to the children.' All of a sudden the candles flared up. The hair on the back of his neck stood up and he got goosebumps all over. Then he went and locked himself in the family room.

"Robert saw a TV special about a man who videotapes ghosts. He wants to try to videotape James. As soon as he talked about it, James got real aggressive and started slamming doors on Robert. I'm not sure how far ghosts can be pushed."

THE CHAIRMAN OF THE BOARD

In Dayton's once-fashionable College Park area stands an attractive stone house built by Edward Parkhurst*, a highly successful banker, for his bride Lucille*. According to local gossip, Lucille sank deeper and deeper into depression because she was unable to have a child. She was given the drugs and shock-treatments common at the time. Nothing helped. Lucille became a crazed, incoherent shell of a woman.

Edward took to drinking heavily. One morning Lucille found him dead in his bed. She ran from neighbor to neighbor, raving and crying, trying to tell them. They all thought she was crazy. It took three days before someone finally understood. Lucille was taken away to a very quiet place.

She was still living there in a kind of twilight when her home was sold to the newly-widowed Mrs. Reardon*. Mrs. Reardon thought the house was lovely, but it upset her already strained nerves to hear someone walking up the stairs, across her room, and over to her bed. Things also went bang and groan and creak in the night. New locks and an intercom system linked to her daughter's house next door reassured her that nothing earthly walked the house. So she began to study her ghost.

He was male, heavy-set, not unfriendly—and worried. He seemed to be wandering, hunting aimlessly. He never spoke to her or touched her, but somehow she knew that he was disappointed to find her in "his" bedroom. Mrs. Reardon didn't smoke, but she began to awake to the odor of cigar smoke. This might have been a dream—except she sometimes found fresh burn marks on the carpet in the morning. She assumed that the ghost was the late Mr. Parkhurst whom she always thought of as "The Chairman of the Board."

Mrs. Reardon's daughter heard the noises and footsteps over the intercom. One weekend when Mrs. Reardon was away, she lost patience and yelled into the intercom, "Your wife doesn't live here anymore, Mr. Parkhurst!"

But that still didn't stop the racket. Disturbances went on for five full years. Then one day Mrs. Reardon's daughter said, "Mom, what's wrong with your house? You haven't had any noises for nearly two weeks."

Mrs. Reardon didn't understand it. She confessed that the house did feel a little lonely. And the next day a neighbor told Mrs. Reardon that Mrs. Parkhurst had died in the nursing home ten days before.[2]

THE SILHOUETTE

In 1972, waiting her turn at the bathroom before school, 13-year-old Tammy sat warming her bare feet at the floor register in the kitchen of her Circleville home. Behind the wall she heard a shushing sound like someone brushing his teeth.

"Only my brother would walk through the house dripping toothpaste everywhere," she thought impatiently, and got up to scold him. Tammy walked around the corner and saw a figure standing in the dark doorway between the family room and the laundry room. Thinking it was her brother, she strode up to the figure with her hands on her hips.

That's when she was enveloped in a patch of icy cold air. With a shock she realized that she could see right through the smoky, man-shaped figure to the sun coming up outside.

"It had substance, yet I could see through it as if it were thick smoke. I don't believe I saw any facial features or colors, just the dark smoky black shape. It seemed to be wearing a dumpy old hat and overcoat. I stared directly at the figure for what seemed at least two minutes, unable to speak, scream or move while my eyes were locked on it. Finally I shut my eyes and ran upstairs to the rest of the family."

"I kept screaming, 'A man, a man! I saw through a man!'"

She was hysterical for several minutes and her mother thought that someone had broken into the house. But all the doors were locked from the inside and there were no footprints in the mud and snow around the house. Tammy's mother tried to convince her that she had been half-asleep and had dreamed the whole thing.

While the family lived in the house, Tammy's parents insisted that she simply had an overactive imagination. But years later Tammy found that her mother, brother, and sisters had all had similar inexplicable experiences. Tammy's older sister would not go into the basement alone, feeling it to be the center of the evil presence, and saw the identical smoky figure of an old man in the doorway to the laundry room four years before Tammy's incident.

Her brother awoke one night to find a black shape of a man standing next to his bed; he felt cold air and evil surrounding the man and without thinking, he jumped out of bed and ran out the second-story window. Fortunately, he landed on the porch roof. Otherwise he would have been killed.

One night when Tammy was sixteen, she awoke to a hair-raising cold and the unearthly howl of her Schnauzer who slept at the foot of her bed. She had heard this "death-howl" before and each time, neighbors had died. Then he yipped loudly and bolted off the bed. Tammy heard him crawling under her younger sister's bed.

Then to her horror she felt her covers, bedspread, and sheets being pulled slowly and deliberately out of her clenched hands and off the foot of the bed. She remembers thinking, "Where are the hands?" at the irresistible force pulling at the edge of the blanket. She screamed and screamed until she lost her voice, but nobody came. Even her sister across the room did not wake up. She sensed a very angry, evil presence around her in the freezing cold and in despair, prepared to die.

It was so unnaturally dark she couldn't see her own hands. But after an eternity, she sensed the presence backing off. The room got noticeably warmer. Somehow she got out of bed and groped her way, arms outstretched, to the light switch, praying that she wouldn't find anything else.

The light showed a wide-open attic door, bedclothes all over the floor, and her sister, who still would not wake though Tammy shook her. The bedroom door was stuck shut. Tammy frantically wrestled with the knob until the door opened. She woke her brother who helped her remake her bed, shut the attic door, and tried to explain it all away. The dog whimpered and wouldn't come out from under her sister's bed until morning.

When Tammy was eighteen the family decided to build a house.

"I became convinced that the spirit did not want me to leave. I felt I was going to die, go insane, or become comatose so my spirit would be trapped in the house. Mom was convinced I was going through a nervous breakdown and stayed awake with me (as much as she could) those last few nights at the house. But as soon as she fell asleep, I felt the evil force smothering me. I believe I survived only by the grace of God."

"In 1987 I did what I'd always dreamed (or had nightmares) of doing. I went back to the old house, introduced myself as someone who grew up in the house, and asked if they had a few minutes to talk. The family enthusiastically invited me in, praising my dad's wonderful remodeling job.

"Casually I asked them if they ever felt they were not alone in the house. They looked at each other for a minute, laughed, and said the neighbors had told them a spooky story of an old woman who once fell down the basement stairs. Actually, they said, only their 10-year-old daughter Suzy* had ever complained, but 'she just had an overactive imagination.'

Suzy constantly complained of strange things happening in her room, cold spots, doors opening/closing by themselves, feeling watched. And she too was afraid of the basement, laundry room, and main bathroom.

"The parents told me that they all made fun of the girl's fears hoping the ridicule would make her grow up. I suggested they try to understand that she honestly believed these scary things were happening to her."

Tammy was relieved to find that Suzy spent part of the year with her mother in another state. The girl said she hated to come back because the house scared her so much. A few months after Tammy's visit, the family moved out.

Tammy found that the evil presence seemed to ignore her during her brief visit. "Maybe whatever was in the house focused so strongly on the adolescent girl that I was not affected. Or, perhaps I've learned to block out my sensitivity to such phenomenon. My brother knows the current residents and they haven't experienced anything unusual. But then, there aren't any young teens in the house now. If there were, I shudder to think what might happen..."

HEADLESS IN HYDE PARK

Hyde Park contains many wonderful old houses set like jewels among the folds of the Cincinnati hills. This particular house had a beautiful view of the Ohio River—and a terrible secret.

About 1975, when the Whites* bought the house, they found clothing and personal items in an apartment above the garage—as if the owner had simply gone away and abandoned everything. The neighbors told them that the previous owner's chauffeur, Morse*, had lived in the apartment until his death in a dreadful auto accident in the 1960s.

Mr. Houston*, his employer, had sent Morse out on a rainy night to pick up a house guest from a local restaurant. Somehow he collided with a car in the opposite lane and, trying to regain control of his car, ran into the guardrail, which rammed through the windshield, decapitating him.

The Whites found Houston's diary among the abandoned papers. It told of his despair and his feelings of terrible responsibility in sending Morse out that night. He became obsessed with the incident, describing the accident in horrific detail over and over and telling how the chauffeur—headless—came to visit him.

He began to find blood on the seat of his new car. He heard a drip, drip, dripping he couldn't explain. Once, he wrote, he opened a car door only to have Morse's head roll out onto his feet, the fresh blood on its face becoming flecked with dirt from the garage floor.

The Whites shuddered at what may have been the ravings of an obsessed madman, but they also knew what they personally had seen: A head—just a head—peering out of the garage apartment windows about dawn. And the head's eyes were open, gazing over the river—over Jordan?[3]**

**This story was collected by "Jeffrey Hawkins" for a book, Cincinnati After Dark. If anyone knows the whereabouts of "Mr. Hawkins" or if he published his book, please contact me at the address on the order blank.

THE SPIRIT OF THE WATERS
Ghosts who walk the waterways

For brief as water falling will be death.
-Conrad Aiken-

Wherever you find water you find ghosts. Running water forms a weak magnetic field, where "ghosts" could be "recorded." English psychic researcher G.W. Lambert wrote that he believed that many ghostly manifestations were caused by the action of underground water—streams, old sewers, tides, floods, or the pressure of water on foundations. He mapped famous cases and demonstrated that poltergeist-type events are more frequent around areas within three miles of tidal water. Whatever the link, here are some spirits that spring from watery graves.

HAUNTED HOLLOW

In 1792 a soldier from what is now Ft. St. Clair went hunting with his dog and was badly wounded by an Indian near the Forty-Foot Pitch. Bleeding heavily, he tried to make his way back to the fort, but fell exhausted at the Garrison Branch. His companions followed the trail of blood to the Haunted Hollow and found him dying. They wanted to carry him back to the fort, but he refused saying, "Let me die here and bury me under these grape vines and bushes; my spirit will haunt this spot for a hundred years."

So the soldiers buried him where he lay, disguising the grave so that the Indians might not find it. The grave has been lost, but the spirit has been seen by many travelers on the West

Road, now Route 122 and walking up and down Garrison Branch and over the old wooden bridge.

He normally appears as a wounded man without a head, but he is sometimes seen with the yellow dog he took hunting.

Strange sounds are also heard in the area of the branch. Travelers heard the screams, moans and sighs of a man in agony. Still others heard a song, coming from the low branches of a tree. Sometimes the man with no head would rise up, as if out of the ground, and jump into the buggies and sleighs of travelers late at night.

One old settler crossed the dry branch at dusk, but on his return after dark, he heard water roaring in the channel. Frightened by its violence, he turned back to town, reporting that the branch was unfordable. Impossible! protested his hearers, no rain had fallen in weeks! He went back to look at the creekbed—it was bone dry and silent.

One interesting thing about this tale is that in England there are countless tales of headless men accompanied by dogs, almost always by a stream or river. If, as some people believe, ghosts are electromagnetic energy, streams would be a natural conductor for these apparitions.[1]

THE GHOST OF THE SCIOTO

When I was a child, the way to my grandparents' home led along the twisting road by the Scioto River in Delaware County. A ruined mill stood on the banks of the river. I looked eagerly for this haunting site, but sometimes the underbrush was so thick it obscured the old brick building. Naively, I wondered if the building could appear and disappear at will.

The river flows quietly beneath limestone cliffs, between banks covered with water or wildflowers in the spring flood season. And once an elegant mansion stood here overlooking the eternally changing river.

In 1825 a man with the improbably simple name of John Robinson stopped for the night at Delaware, at that time scarcely more than a few log cabins, a blacksmith shop, stable, and tavern. Robinson didn't drink with the rest of the travelers

or swap stories about bears and panthers, but the next day hired
a horse and set off for south Delaware County.

Calling at a farm, Robinson arrogantly told the man that he
wanted to buy his land. Not liking Robinson's looks or
manners, the farmer set an absurdly high price on the farm. To
his amazement, the stranger didn't flinch and paid in gold—
Spanish *reals*.

Ignoring the inevitable whispers, Robinson began to
design a magnificent house to stand atop a cliff overlooking the
Scioto. Wagonloads of craftsmen from the Eastern coast began
to arrive. Stones were blasted out of the limestone cliffs lining
the riverbanks and mortared into place.

The powerfully-built Robinson himself felled oaks and
then, with an unexpectedly delicate touch, carved paneling and
overmantels. Each one of the dozen rooms held some master-
piece of his carving. Robinson also built a tomb for himself of
cut stone—a large tomb, as though he expected others to be
joining him.

More wagons arrived—this time laden with furniture
swaddled in straw, imported from abroad. Those who unloaded the wagons told of brocade sofas, and massive sideboards laden with plate, and crystal chandeliers.

The whole county was abuzz. Mothers dreamed of
Robinson asking to dance with their daughters at the housewarming ball he would hold. The daughters whispered that
while Robinson could freeze anyone with one of his fierce
looks, he was *too* mysterious and romantic. They speculated
that he was the youngest son of an English lord who'd gotten
himself into some scrape. And money could make up for a lot
of fierce looks.

Certainly he seemed to have plenty of money. He also
gave himself lordly airs for as soon as the last workman
departed, he bolted the heavy door and no callers were admitted. Then tongues wagged in earnest. A local workman,
brought in to repair a piece of broken furniture, reported seeing
Robinson at work in his studio, painting fabulous paintings
And in that studio, taking up an entire wall, he said, his voice

suddenly hushed, hung the most fabulous picture of all. It showed the deck of a ship crowded with pirates surrounding their captain in a gold-laced coat. The captain was Robinson.

Those eager mothers now mentally drew their skirts back from this foul scourge of the Scioto whose ill-gotten wealth had built a house of blood. But Robinson didn't lack for female companionship. One day—no one had seen her arrive—neighbors glimpsed a beautiful young woman in the woods. She could have been a Spanish *infanta* with her ebony hair and eyes; her exquisite olive skin. It was whispered that he had captured her entire family on one of his cruises and murdered all of them except for the daughter. She was small, with child-like bones, and wandered the summer woods whenever she was not posing for Robinson in his studio. She loved to sit on the cliff and look at the river drifting by, perhaps thinking of it running to the great ocean she had crossed. Or of her home in some sunnier place. No one ever heard her speak—only her shrill cries as Robinson beat her, for he had a vicious temper. But no one wanted to interfere with a man like Robinson. And soon winter closed around the mansion.

When spring finally came and the river ran mud-colored, Robinson and the girl were nowhere to be seen. The windows of the mansion remained dark; growing darker as spring advanced and the forest vines crawled over the glass.

No one dared approach the house until midsummer when a group of men, making enough noise to raise the dead, knocked on the iron-bound front door, then battered down the door with a log. Room after room stood empty of life. All was in order—except the library. There slashed canvases were strewn about like corpses. Chairs and tables were overturned; some dark liquid had spattered the walls. And from a dark dried pool on the floor, handprints smeared their way up the wall to a portrait of the Spanish girl.

As the men looked at the canvas, its fresh colors seemed to come to life, as if the girl was imprisoned in the frame and was trying to find her way out. The eyes moved, following them, then the lips parted as if to speak. But the men heard only a sob. They broke and ran back to Delaware.

The villagers avoided the house for only a few weeks. Greed soon replaced fear and men battered at the walls with sledgehammers, tore the paneling away with picks. In the end the mansion was like a dismembered body, gaping wounds in its walls and foundations, the lead skinned from its roof, and the beautiful woodwork scarred and bruised.

No man ever found so much as a single gold coin. Robinson's fabled treasure had vanished—like the man himself. The house decayed quickly—unnaturally so, said the villagers. For many years the story was told by firesides, until Robinson was transmuted into a wizard, a servant of the Evil One, fetched away at last, with his ill-gotten gains.

But true stories were told of the spirit of the Spanish lady. On late summer afternoons, she could be seen flitting through the forest in her stiff brocade gown, her face shrouded in lace. She would sit on her stone chair overlooking the river, then glide to the remains of the mansion, the stone blocks jutting through the mossy overgrowth like the bones of a dead giant. There she would throw herself onto the ground, sobbing hopelessly. And in the dying sunlight her ghostly body would dissolve into the forest floor, as her earthly body decayed in an unknown grave.

Today nothing remains of Robinson House, now on private property in Concord Township. Only a crypt—empty except for snakes and salamanders seeking the damp coolness of the grave.[2]

DEATH TAKES A DIVE

Amy Mundhenk was my kind of witness, combining an observant eye for detail coupled with a quirky sense of humor. She told this story about Springfield's old Y:

This happened in early fall of 1989. I was going with a guy named Bill. Bill's roommate, Wayne, liked to chase after the supernatural. He was the kind of guy who would play chicken with farm tractors. If he parked on a Cry Baby Bridge at midnight—he'd get run over.

Wayne said there were lots of ghosts at the Springfield Y, which had been closed for several years. "Let's go look for them!" he said.

My first reaction was, "Yeah, right! let's go get arrested for trespassing." But, since I had nothing better to do, I went along.

Bill packed his sword and a couple of flashlights. When we got there, we went through a broken window into the boiler room. Walking around in this big dark place with flashlights, we could see that the place had obviously been used by crack smokers. I was less worried about ghosts than something would collapse or fall on us or we would get arrested. Wayne took the lead. He kept going, "Oooh, do you see that? Do you see that?"

We climbed to the floor with the swimming pool. It was empty except for debris. The area felt weird, creepy. People had drawn occult symbols on walls and there were burned-out candles lying around. It really had a bad psychic feel. There was also a smell in the pool area: mold or mildew or dirt. I got the feeling that there was a lot going on at the pool, that it was sort of a homeless shelter for disenfranchised spirits that hadn't found their way to the Light.

Wayne was running around in the bottom of the pool. After he climbed out, I pointed my my flashlight at it. Now it was full of water and there was a dead guy floating in it.

He was face down, dark hair, white skin, average build, wearing swim trunks. There was blood on the water. I couldn't see a head wound; I just remember seeing blood coming out of his head.

I said, "Bill, do you see that?"

He didn't. Wayne didn't. Some people can't see spirits even when they're right in front of them. It scared me to death!

"Bill, let's leave!" I begged.

"There's nothing to be afraid of," Bill scoffed. And he and Wayne dragged me into the locker room. There I heard people laughing and talking and whispering. As we were standing there I said to Bill, "Somebody else just came in." We were three floors away from where we'd climbed in the window.

"Probably crack smokers," Bill said

"No, it's not," I insisted.

Bill pulled out his sword; Wayne had a metal pipe. We went back out to the pool and the guy was gone. Then we went up a flight of stairs and saw flashlights.

"Who's there?" said a voice.

"Adventurers!" Bill said boldly, "Who are you?"

"Springfield police," the voice answered, "Please come out with your hands up."

Sitting in the cruiser, I told the police about the body in the pool. They thought I was a complete fruitcake. They didn't even go and look. They said they never heard of anybody ever dying there. We told the cops the truth about what we had been doing. They looked at each other, then called the church that owned the property. The church people said, "Let them go."

That was the last time I let Bill and Wayne talk me into anything like that!"

The Y has been torn down and turned into a parking lot. But I wonder: If you parked there late at night would you see the ghostly floater bobbing face-down in mid-air?

THE GHOST RIDER OF HENRY COUNTY

On hot summer afternoons as thunderstorms roll across the plains of northwestern Ohio, and bolts of lightning slam into the earth of the Black Swamp, a black-caped rider on a brown horse bolts by the Henry County cemetery. They turn down the road to the river and there they disappear.

The ghostly pair have been seen at least ten times by a resident who lives near the cemetery. She says they always appear from nowhere, ride like devil was after them, and disappear at the river.

Local residents wonder if the ghost-rider was riding to catch a ferry at the old crossing when he got caught in a summer storm. Some think he and his horse were struck by lightning and now spend eternity trying to beat the storm.

According to tradition, supernatural beings can not cross water. The river might be preventing the spectral horseman from reaching his home. Or could it be that he is waiting for Charon, ghostly ferry-man of Hell, to row him across?

The real mystery is the experience of a Toledo contractor digging sand from land next to the cemetery. As his daughter later told a local ghost-watcher, he was baffled by the hoof-prints in the sand, since he hadn't seen any horses for miles.[3]

THE DELTA QUEEN

Does the *Delta Queen,* that paddle-wheeler passenger boat plying the Ohio and Mississippi Rivers, have a crew member not listed on its manifest?

"There is talk of it," said Ann, one of 75 crew members on the *Delta Queen.*

The extra member, some suggest, is the ghost of Mary Greene, whose family began working the river in the early 1800s.

She had her master's license before her first son was born in 1898. She died on the *Delta Queen* in 1950 at the age of 83.

"They say she 'visits' the bar on the Texas deck. And breaks glasses," said Ann. "When she was on the boat, drinking wasn't allowed. The bar was a library."

Could boat vibrations, however minimal, have caused the glasses to inch toward the shelf edge and topple?

Ann said that COULD be so.

But she points to other incidents.

"Things keep disappearing from the cabin where she died," said Ann, "The cabins can all be locked when we're in port, no way to get in, but when passengers get to that room, they find the towels have disappeared."

Also, one crew member said he once felt the "presence" of Mrs. Greene, but never actually saw her.

"He said it was a windless night on the river, and everyone was sitting in the lounge," Ann explained, "The starboard door opened and closed by itself. Then after a minute, the port side door did, too, as if someone had walked through."

Just Captain Mary Greene making her rounds to see that all is ship-shape.[4]

THE TUNNEL

Kelleys Island is named for Datus Kelley, the man who helped the island boom in the 1840s after the limestone quarry was opened on the western end of the island.

The quarrymen were often Italian immigrants. They spoke Italian and went to Mass. The foreman and the paymaster were usually Protestants from Sandusky. There was bad blood between the two groups and fights often broke out.

Irritated by this friction, the foreman ordered the quarrymen to work faster, even forcing them to work the dangerous night shift when a man couldn't see well enough to safely set a blasting charge. The Italians retaliated by getting drunk on their days off and singing raucously through the streets of the village. Furious, the foreman ordered more overtime, faster deliveries, and more risks for the dynamite crews. For ten straight days the crews slaved around the clock, digging and boring, blasting and drilling. Deeper and deeper they went, tunneling under the lake.

Finally the foreman made a fatal mistake. He ordered the chief dynamiter, "Big Pepe" Battaglia, to blast away a rock shelf that overhung a quarry filled with water. Pepe argued, and fought, and finally cursed the foreman as he pushed the plunger.

The rock shelf—tons of rock—plummeted into the water, causing a huge wave to roll out of the cut, sweeping away Pepe and dozens of other men. Most of the bodies were never found.

It was after that that the mysterious shipwrecks began. Sailors on the ships carrying the huge chunks of limestone across to Marblehead began to tell of terrifying groans rising from the water at night. They claimed that Pepe and his men had tunneled all the way from the Kelleys Island quarry to the Marblehead quarry west of the old lighthouse. And they said that Pepe and his men marched up and down those dank tunnels at night, their hands bound with chains dragging behind them like a scum of silver foam on the water.

They also said that the ghosts of the drowned quarrymen had sworn vengeance on the ships and the sailors and the quarry operators. When a ship went down, it was because angry ghosts had thrown a loop of chain around the ship's propeller, dragging it down without a trace. And the drowned sailors were forced to join the crew of ghosts shuffling for eternity through the slime-walled tunnel beneath Lake Erie.

The Lake is well-known for the violence of its autumn storms, for the mysterious disappearance of many vessels. Skeptics say the sheer unpredictability of the weather accounts for many lost ships. And ships loaded with many tons of limestone would naturally sink quickly with few survivors.

Sandusky-area writer Russell Ramsey first heard the tunnel story at Camp Hartnung, a retreat for the boys of the Grace Episcopal Church Choristers. A tale told to frighten impressionable lads around the campfire? Or to keep them away from the dangerous, water-filled quarries? But Russell's research turned up the story of the *Sand Merchant*, wrecked on October 19, 1936. Nineteen crew members drowned. The five survivors babbled senselessly about waves that groaned and pulled at their overturned lifeboat like ghostly hands. As late as the 1980s, Ramsey was told by an elderly Island resident, "Why don't you write about the ghosts that live in this here quarry! They walk at night through tunnels to Marblehead."

Ramsey and his family laughed. But that night it stormed and the next day they read in the *Sandusky Register* about two boats that were wrecked on the rocks, coming home from Kelleys Island.

A coincidence? Possibly. But there are those who swear that you can hear the howling of lost souls in the rising wind and that vengeful ghosts still walk—down below, where the dead men go.[5]

THE SHOW MUST GO ON—
AND ON...
More theatre ghosts

Bring down the curtain, the farce is played out...
-Francois Rabelais, last words-

THE CLAGUE PLAYHOUSE GHOST

Westlake's Clague Playhouse was literally born in a barn. Conditions were challenging when the theatre group moved into the barn in 1967—there were chickens in the rafters. And when Dale Bugos joined the group in 1981 there were already stories about "Walter," the resident ghost, supposedly the original owner of the property. Whenever anything got misplaced or an accident happened, the mishap was laughingly blamed on Walter.

Some members, however, took it seriously—refusing to be in the building alone or go into the cellar where props were stored. Dale had his share of minor mishaps—odd noises, losing things and then finding them in unlikely places. But these could be explained away. What wasn't so easy to explain was the uneasy feeling of being watched. Still, there didn't seem to be any common thread to the occurrences. Dale felt he really didn't have any rational reason to believe in "Walter." Until he decided to clean out the attic.

The attic, which had been hayloft, office space, and light booth, was crammed so full Dale literally had to climb over piles of costumes and furniture to get to the other end. He organized a cleaning party, dumped everything through a trap door onto the stage, and took the next week to fix up the attic.

He was too busy at first to notice the familiar feeling of being watched although he constantly misplaced his tools. That, coupled with irritation at noises that sounded like kids throwing rocks against the building, upset him. It was a warm day and he decided to call it quits. To finish, he arranged some prop cups and saucers on shelves at the end of the room, then began sweeping the floor. As he bent over to sweep the dust into the dustpan, a teacup crashed on the floor behind his feet. His temper flared as he turned to see what else he'd hit with the broom handle—then he saw that he was a good fifteen feet from the china and realized the cup had been thrown by an unseen hand.

Dale saw red. "I just finished that!" he yelled, "Leave me alone!" Immediately it was as if someone had turned up the lights and a feeling of heaviness vanished.

After that, Dale found that saying something like, "All right, stop it now!" out loud would bring things to a halt. And he noticed that Walter became active only when permanent changes like shelves or costume racks were being added to the building. Dale thought he had finally found the thread.

But this certainty didn't last. Dale was painting the lobby by himself and he just couldn't shake his feeling of uneasiness. "Walter, leave me alone," he asked out loud. The feeling got so bad that he went to call a friend over to keep him company. As he was talking to her, he heard a crash in the lobby and ran to investigate.

Dale found the stepladder on its side with the paint pan and roller lying right-side up on the floor. Surprisingly, very little paint had spilled, but it was enough to make Dale blow his stack. He screamed at Walter for about five minutes, telling the ghost to go away and never bother him again!

And after that he was never bothered physically except by the feeling of being watched. About seven years ago some burst pipes damaged the theatre so badly that most of it had to be completely rebuilt. Dale thought that the renovations would have sent Walter on a rampage, but it seems to have had the opposite effect—Dale hasn't even felt the presence since the fall of 1991. Perhaps, he says, the many changes disoriented Walter completely and he gave up the ghost.

Postscript: After Dale wrote out this story, he was alone in the theatre, editing a sound effects tape. There were strange noises with no explanation and the feeling was back. Has Walter returned for an encore?

THE THEATRE OF THE MIND

It was a chill, overcast summer day in 1993 when Rosi and Anne and I drove up the tree-shadowed drive to the Ohio Veteran's Children's Home. We drove past the administration building, turreted like an armory; past the fountain, the bandshell, and many-boarded up buildings. Once, six hundred children lived at the Home. Most remembered the Home fondly all their lives. Now it is home to perhaps one hundred troubled children. Allegations involving money and abuse keep cropping up and every few years there is talk of shutting the Home down.

I parked the car in front of the Julian R. Rooney Memorial Hall and we huddled on the porch out of the brisk wind. The slate flooring was crumbling under our feet.

The buildings on either side of the auditorium had half-buried windows in the foundation, giving them a sinking look, like old tombstones. From the building next door, Donna, who teaches at the Home, hurried over to unlock the door.

Even with marble wall panels and fancy portholed doors to the auditorium, the echoing lobby was shabby, like an opera house now given over to peep shows. Fake palm trees from the previous Towne Square Players production, *South Pacific*, were stacked like cordwood at the back of the theatre. The room was surprising long and narrow, with two aisles that swept us up toward the stage, set for *The Sound of Music*. And up there, something waited on stage.

I avoided looking at it, looking instead at the bare cement floor beneath my feet, the tall windows curtained in red, the children sitting in rows in their seats—all freshly-scrubbed faces, clip-on ties, hair bows, and pigtails. The auditorium was packed with well-behaved children, who, judging from their clothing, were from the 1950s. They looked expectantly at me and the stage, waiting for the program to start.

I followed the others up the steps to the backstage area. At the top of the stairs, I felt very weak in the knees. I walked over the stage as quickly as possible. There was a cold spot at stage left.

Going back to the steps to the basement, we all smelled a foul odor wafting up the stairs. Beneath the stage, in the narrow basement hall, we walked past rows of grim little rooms like prison cells. There was a bad smell throughout the hall and rooms, like rotting fruit. It wasn't the plumbing and it moved around. On the floor of the farthest room lay a wooden platform with a sheet on it. Any minute I expected to find a body.

As we re-emerged from the basement, the children were still in their seats. Someone was standing by the third row—a ghostly usherette waiting to show us to our seat with a little ectoplasmic flashlight?

Upstairs was even chillier. The end room, with a view overlooking the campus, was unusually cold. Poking into the empty closet, I heard the words, "Hanged, hanged..." At last we found some chairs and sat in the chilly lobby to talk with Donna.

"I'm afraid," she admitted, "People are injured here constantly. And they seem to be influenced by the building. There's a lot of cast tension. People start to hate each other— there are some very bad vibes between people who don't normally act that way."

Shirley Ellis, artistic director of the Towne Square Players, says there were an unusual number of leg accidents and injuries starting with *South Pacific*, the majority of which occurred on the same spot on stage—the cold spot. "At one point we had six people on crutches."

Various students, Shirley, and her daughter Elizabeth have seen a white figure in the light booth.

"I saw what looked like a woman with long hair," Shirley told me, "It moved fairly quickly and seemed to have white robes on. It glowed in a ghostly white light. I went upstairs to see what could be causing it. There was nothing." Shirley and other cast members also reported hearing invisible children laughing and playing, singing a nursery song.

Reportedly there have been several deaths in the building: One woman dancing on stage fell and broke her neck. As two boys were playing in the projection room, one boosted the other up to one of the windows—the boy fell into the auditorium and died. The other boy hanged himself. Another story, possibly only a rumor, says that while the stage was being built, the foreman fell to his death.

We all took a final look at the theatre. The auditorium would have been full in the 1950s—it is still full. "Those people have left something behind," said Donna quietly.

Before we left, we walked over to look at the pathetic little tombstones in the graveyard. The newest is a wooden cross marked with the name of a young man who had gone from the Home to a career in show business. He died in his twenties.

"All these young lives," said Rosi, shaking her head "cut tragically short..."

But they still live on—in the theatre of the mind.

A BONE TO PICK

In Cincinnati's historic Music Hall, the balconies are held up by slender pillars modeled on femurs, and the narrow seats seem designed for more skeletal occupants than the robust German music-lovers of early Cincinnati. And in 1988 workers drilling a new elevator shaft beneath Cincinnati's Music Hall hit a different kind of pay dirt when they unearthed over two hundred pounds of bones—the skeletal remains of men, women and children buried in a crude cement crypt.

Dirty doings at the Music Hall? Surely these couldn't all be the bones of people who talked during the soft movements? To tell the story, we must return to 1821, when Cincinnati's first public hospital—the Commercial Hospital & Lunatic Asylum—was established on what was then the fringes of the city.

The Cincinnati WPA Guide described the hospital thus: "Wretched conditions prevailed. The stench was intolerable; the insane, chained to the floors, screamed night and day; and so many patients died that the superintendent was nicknamed 'Absalom Death.'"

Poor patients who died there were buried in the Potter's Field, the cemetery for paupers, suicides and strangers, where Music Hall stands today. Many of the dead came from the Pest House—an "isolation ward" where patients with TB, cholera, smallpox, and terminal poverty were sent to reduce the surplus population. The bodies were bundled underground without ceremony or coffins. Coffins cost money and thrifty middle-class Germans didn't see the point of wasting money on the improvident dead.

In 1870 the city allowed a German singing society to build a tin-roofed wooden building, known as Saengerfeste Hall, on the grounds. Stories of hauntings were immediate and wide-spread, but didn't stop the May Music Festivals from being held there. In 1876, work was begun on a new, larger permanent Music Hall building and it was then that the first skeletons came to light.

Lafcadio Hearn, who relished every sordid moment, set the scene with his usual nasty-minded flair in the *Cincinnati Commercial* for October 22, 1876:.

"This rich yellow soil, fat with the human flesh and bone and brain it has devoured, is being disemboweled by a hundred spades and forced to exhibit its ghastly secrets to the sun...you will behold small Golgothas—mingled piles of skulls, loose vertebrae, fibulas, tibias and the great curving bones of the thigh....All are yellow, like the cannibal clay which denuded them of their fleshly masks...Bone after bone...is turned over with a scientific application of kicks...dirty fingers are poked into empty eyesockets...ribs crack in pitiful remonstrance to reckless feet; and tobacco juice is carelessly squirted among the decaying skulls....by night there come medical students to steal the poor skulls."

It was then, said Hearn, that the unearthed dead began to walk.

Shadowy people wandered through the halls by night, walking softly behind the night watchmen and terrifying them with strange creaking noises in the rafters or the sound of heavy bodies plummeted from the roof to the floor. There were ghostly knockings—let me in! let me in!—but no one ever stood at the door when it was opened. Dogs brought into the building would whine to be let out, eyes bulging and ears laid back with terror. The invisible folk were especially restless in damp weather, but not during concerts or balls, as if the living overpowered them. But after each intermission, the noises came back, louder than ever.

The building also housed various public fairs. One morning an exhibitor saw a young woman standing by his booth. She was tall and fair and blonde, dressed in the fashion of his grandmother's day and there was something about her pale figure that made him want a closer look. But as he stepped forward, the figure became transparent and a wintery chill passed over him. Hearn wrote: "The tall woman had been sepulchered under the yellow clay below the planking upon which he stood; and the worms had formed the wedding-rings of Death about her fingers half a century before...."

Throughout the years, the bones were never allowed to rest in pieces, but kept being resurrected from the basement. In 1927 a half dozen skeletons were placed in a cement crypt and forgotten until 1969, when Music Hall was being remodeled. Construction workers found the bones as they put arch supports in the basement to hold up the auditorium floor. They built another concrete chest to hold the bones. The chest then was placed at the foot of the freight elevator shaft where it was uncovered again in 1988 as the shaft for the elevator was deepened. Oddly enough, night watchmen have reported hearing the tinkling strains of a music box as they pass the freight elevator at night. The source can never be found.

Hearn was right when he said, "Is it likely that the ghosts will be driven away from their old resting places merely because some of their bones are removed? Who dares guess how deeply that soil is permeated with the substance of the dead?..."

As I wrote this story I kept hearing the "Fossils" section from *The Carnival of the Animals*, by Camille Saint-Saens, a sprightly, clattering piece played on the jolly bones of the xylophone. But perhaps a more appropriate tune would be the phrase from Handel's *Messiah*: "And the dead shall be raised—incorruptible...."[1]

THE PHANTOM OF THE OPERA HOUSE

Built in 1841, the building known as "The Opera House" was the first Methodist Church in Trumbull County. It was moved twice, once in 1865 across Cortland and then in 1879, when it was moved just a few hundred feet to its present location. In 1882 it was purchased by Solomon Kline and his wife Elizabeth who renamed it Kline's Hall.

Dorothy Klein and her late husband Erwin worked for the Bazetta-Cortland Historical Society, ushering groups of visitors through the restored building and telling of its long history. These tours always concluded with a brief concert on an historic Chickering square grand piano.

On a dreary, drizzly day in 1987, Erwin had just seen the last visitor out the door. He did a final check of the building, locking the doors, turning out the lights in the lower level, then walking up the back stairs to the auditorium. His hat and raincoat were in the storage room, along with about two hundred folding chairs and forty folding tables. As Erwin crossed the auditorium, he heard a tremendous, crash-bang-thump! as if all two hundred chairs had dominoed to the floor at once.

"How lucky can you be?" Erwin thought to himself crossly, "Everyone else has gone home and you get to pick up and restack all those chairs and tables that have fallen over!"

Reluctantly he opened the door and turned on the lights. Not a single table or chair was out of place.

"Since my mother never raised any dummies," said Erwin, "I took my hat and coat, went out the back door, locked it and drove home. Knowing no wife would ever give credence to such a story, I simply said nothing about it to Dorothy."

Then, one day, his wife had a fright of her own. Like Erwin, Dorothy had been the last one out of the building after a Historical Society meeting. "As I came up the back stairs, I heard heavy footsteps going across the floor of the auditorium. But I had already checked and there was no one here but me."

Dorothy fled home, where she and Erwin compared notes. Several months later, Kathy Cline, another Historical Society member, confided to Dorothy that whenever she was in the building alone, she heard a man talking, but couldn't quite make out the words.

Erwin and Dorothy decided that only people whose names sounded like Klein would notice anything strange at the Opera House.

"We came to the conclusion that it's Solomon Kline walking around his Opera House checking to see what we're doing here, so we have named him the Phantom of the Opera House."

But the story doesn't end there.

In 1992 as a group tour was leaving, a well-dressed lady came to Erwin and said, "You know, all the time that lady was playing the piano, I heard the most beautiful woman's voice singing!"

Erwin thought, "That couldn't be Solomon—could it be that Elizabeth has joined him?

"I told Dorothy and she caught up to the lady as she was about to board the bus. Among other things she found out that the woman's name was Mrs. Small. So much for our theory about only people named Klein-Cline-Kline hearing things in the Opera House. Then we remembered—Do you know the German word for small? *Kleine*."

TWYLA

Otterbein students call her Twyla (or Twila) Tharp, just like the famous choreographer. But unlike her brilliant namesake, Twyla was a failure. She was a moody, unattractive girl, who desperately wanted to be a star. Armed with minimal talent, however, she never got a single part she auditioned for. Whenever she tried out for anything, she always got put in the back row, second spear carrier from the left.

After one last, spectacularly unsuccessful audition, Twyla stayed behind after everyone else had gone home. In tears, she climbed up to the scenery rigging.

"I'll show them, I'll show them," she muttered and then dove to her death on the stage below.

Apparently even her death was a flop. College Archivist Melinda Gilpin says that there is no record of anyone named Twyla Tharp ever enrolled at Otterbein. She adds that there is also no record of anyone ever dying in Cowan Hall, which was built in 1951. To hard-headed, pragmatic types, this might seem irrefutable evidence that there is no ghost at Cowan. But just ask the theatre students who claim that, resentful of anyone in the theatre, she comes back to terrorize anyone alone in the building after dark.

Doors bang open and shut when no one else is in the building.

Students slip on the spot on stage where Twyla supposedly landed.

If the building is very quiet, you can hear Twyla crying.

Students wearing headsets backstage have reported hearing a family quarreling over the radios.

Just two hours before a Campus Center Theatre performance of *Stepping Out*, lighting designer Rob Johnson discovered that about ninety carefully programmed lighting cues had disappeared from the computerized lighting board.

Johnson never programmed so many cues "from scratch" so quickly. The show opened only a few minutes late.

But was the mishap a product of computer, human—or

ghostly—error? Anyone with a flair for the dramatic will prefer the latter theory.

"Whenever anything goes wrong at Cowan Hall, we traditionally blame it on Twyla the Theatre Ghost," Johnson said. "She must have crossed campus to wreak havoc on our board."

It sounds like a typically Twyla thing to do: if she can't be in the play, nobody will get to see it.[2]

WESLEY, THE GHOST OF WESTWOOD

"Wesley" was the caretaker of Westwood Town Hall, before Westwood was absorbed by Cincinnati. He lived in a tiny basement apartment in the building but after the merger, he was fired and told to vacate the building. In despair, Wesley hung himself in the back stairs leading to his apartment.

Today the building is a center for recreation and community theatre including the Cincinnati Young People's Theatre. Michael Berger worked with the group in 1988.

He said, "I have never felt totally comfortable in the building. I am not usually frightened, but before I had ever heard of Welsey, I would get strange feelings in certain rooms: sometimes feelings of being watched, sometimes a feeling of 'dryness,' like dust being poured over me. I also felt that it would be unwise to enter certain rooms at certain times. I never felt danger, just a feeling of, 'Never mind, I can do this another time.'"

Michael's first run-in with Wesley was in the fall of 1985. He was in charge of props for the Agatha Christie mystery, *Ten Little Indians.*

"After each show, I would replace the props where they belonged. When I returned each morning with the person who unlocked the building, I would find the props deliberately rearranged. No one had any motive for messing things up. This went on for the whole run of the show."

A young woman who worked on costumes came in one night to find all the carefully arranged costumes in total disarray. One costume even disappeared and they later found it hidden outside the building.

In the early 1986, Winnie*, a 14-year old friend of Michael's was studying in the basement cafeteria, near the same area where Wesley had his apartment. One of the serving windows, which have heavy, roll-down metal partitions, was down, locked into a ring in the countertop. Suddenly the handle flipped up and the metal partition shot up as if thrown. A few minutes later a door slammed.

Winnie sighed and said to him, "Wesley, calm down. OK, you're here, but I'm studying and I'd like you to leave me alone, I've got work to do." All was quiet for her after that.

"In December 1988, after a performance of *A Christmas Carol*, me and my friend Chris Quitter locked up the building and went to a Christmas party. When I returned him to the parking lot to pick up his car, we sat and talked for a while. The building was dark except for the single spotlight in the parking lot and a small security light visible through the ground level windows. I happened to glance in the rear-view mirror. I did a classic double-take and my jaw dropped.

"Standing in the basement window, holding the cafeteria curtains aside with one arm, was the figure of a man watching us. He was standing between the light source inside and the window frame and blocked out the light as a solid figure would. We had personally locked up the building, and I knew for certain that no one was inside.

"Quietly I told Chris to move the side mirror so he could see behind the car.

"'What do you see?' I asked him, without explaining.

"'There's a dark form standing in the window holding the curtain back,' he said, adding, 'We locked up; there's nobody in there....'

"We were afraid to move. The man watched us for about 20-25 minutes. We sat frozen, both out of fear that he would vanish and purely out of fear for ourselves. Finally he turned away and the curtain fell back in place.

"I don't know what Wesley is. Personally, I've always felt he's still taking care of the building. He seems to watch the goings-on, checks up on people who are there late to make sure they aren't causing trouble, tells people when its time to leave. I almost feel that if you messed with the building, you'd get hurt. I always say hello and goodbye to Wesley when I enter the main auditorium and that seems to make the room better. You feel cold, you feel chills, but nobody's there...."

CALL FOR DOCTOR DEATH
Haunted hospitals and clinics

Pale death, the grand physician, cures all pain.
-John Clare-

I've often wondered why hospitals aren't more often haunted. Perhaps there is a special class of hospital angels who help the recent dead move along. Ghosts have been driven away by electrifying basements or attics. The sheer amount of electricity in hospitals might create a kind of ghost-zapper. Wouldn't it be ironic if the very technology that prolongs life, drives spirits into the afterlife?

SPIRITS ON CALL

I worked at Doctors Hospital on Austin Avenue in Perry Heights from 1972 to 1981, [wrote Marilyn*]. In those years, I experienced a few things myself and heard many more accounts.

When I first started working at the hospital, I worked with four other women in the pediatrics division on the midnight shift. One night as we were doing routine paperwork, a very strange thing happened. There was a bathroom for employees directly across from the nurses' station—in plain view of everyone. All of a sudden the water came on full blast in the sink. Since I seemed to be the only one bothered, I asked the other staff members. One replied, "You'll just have to get used to it, it's our resident ghost."

One nurse talked of a night that still haunts her. The nurses' locker room used to be in the basement, back by the

morgue hallway. She put her things in her locker and was on
her way up the stairs when she heard someone call her name.
She turned around to answer, only to see an empty hallway.
She started up the steps again, and heard her name, even
louder. It sounded like it was coming from under the stairwell.
Figuring it was a friend trying to play a trick on her, she walked
back down the steps and turned towards the stairwell. Then she
stopped, not quite believing what she saw.

In the corner was a white vapor and as she watched, it
started to take human form. She finally got up the courage to
move and ran up the stairs. All she says about the incident is
that she is now a believer in ghosts and she never goes to the
locker room alone anymore.

One extremely snowy night, several of the staff called in to
say that they were snowed in and couldn't make it to work. To
cover the shortage, people were pulled from other divisions and
everyone was extremely busy. Towards morning, one nurse
came out of the back hall and remarked, "I'm really glad that
they sent the extra nurse's aide to help out."

"What are you talking about?" asked the Charge Nurse,
"No one sent us an aide."

"Well, she's back there making beds. Can't you hear her
humming?"

The Charge Nurse listened for a minute then said, "Oh.
She's back."

When pressed to explain, she said, "We used to have an
aide who hummed all the time when she did her work. One
night while making beds she died of a heart attack. Every now
and then when things get really hectic around here, she comes
back to help out."

There is also a room in the hospital that was supposedly
cursed by an elderly woman patient. It is said that she told the
nurses if they let her die in that room, no one would be able to
stay there again.

Shortly after this the old woman did die. Patients began to
complain of the severe cold in the room. A few people rang the
nurses' station to tell of a confused older patient trying to take

their covers off and telling them to get out of her bed. One patient demanded to be moved.

"How can I sleep," he demanded, "when that old lady stands there laughing and carrying on?"

Supposedly the hospital administrator, who had been admitted for some routine tests asked to be given this room—to see if the complaints were valid. At 2 a.m. he came out of the room, deathly-pale, and gave orders that no more patients were to be put in that room. A few days later the room was sealed off. It was even rumored that a priest was brought in to bless the hospital....

Marilyn ended her letter, "I do believe that spirits do linger, if only for a little while. But, maybe, some are here for eternity...."

OF MISTS AND MORGUES

The timbered and turreted house that stands by the Dayton hospital looks like a typical haunted house. In fact, it is. Workmen and security guards have reported hearing footsteps and heavy furniture shifts up in the attic, where no one has any reason to be.

But the most well-known hauntings at this hospital aren't in this eerie-looking building, but in the modern, well-lit, antiseptic, and, one would think, ghost-free, areas of the former nurses' training school and in the very hospital itself.

In the 1950s and 60s the site of the Center for Health Education was used as the nursing students' residence. Students and security guards saw strange shadows silhouetted on the gym wall.

An old surgeon in green scrubs has also been seen in the lower levels of the hospitals. One nursing student says she accidentally walked right through him.

Then there's the fifth floor.... One evening, Wren*, a nurse at the hospital in the early 1980s was changing a bed with another nurse on the fifth floor. As they quietly talked and laughed, she just happened to look up at the door of the room across the hall. A misty thing stood there—as tall and wide as the whole door, swaying back and forth.

Wren was so shocked she could hardly talk. "Look, look, look, look," she babbled to the other nurse whose back was to the door. And as soon as Wren spoke, the thing slid right into the door, dissolving like mist. Wren ran across the hall, but there was nothing there.

Other nurses, who didn't know Wren, have told me of seeing the same tall, swaying, misty figure on the fifth floor. Another told of sitting at her station on five and seeing a elderly woman's death-white face reflected in the dark window in front of her. She screamed and buzzed the nurse out on the floor to come quickly. "I can't come right now," replied the nurse. Her patient, an elderly woman, had just died.

Karen* worked for nearly three years in the hospital's billing office.

"It used to be the morgue," she told me, "We always said they just took out the bodies, put down carpet, and painted the walls."

There were definite cold and warm spots which moved around. And there were really bad odors—only nobody could find anything to account for them.

"And we had a—little prankster," Karen said hesitantly. "The main thing he did was throw papers in the air—trying to scare you. He would wait until people were staying on alone after work. Then papers would look like they were being picked up, held at about neck-height, and then flutter down. Sometimes they would actually fountain off the desk.

"He would open and shut a desk drawer and rustle papers in the next cubicle. You'd walk over there, and nobody was there. We sensed that it was a male. He harassed one woman in particular. Finally she said, 'I'm not scared! Stop it!' After that he didn't bother her again."

THE CLINIC

Although it was a sunny day, the clinic in Fairborn was undeniably dark. It was nearly brand-new, with modern mauve-print wallpaper, trendy frosted glass wall sconces, and comfortable waiting room furniture, but it was *dark*. I was running about 10 minutes late and I was taken aback by the deserted waiting room. I went up to the sliding glass door at the receptionist's desk and looked at three angry, set faces: Carol, Patty*, and Bernadette*.

"Uh oh," I thought, "they're mad at me for being late. They hate me."

But later Patty told me, "You feel like a different person when you sit at that window. Anger and hostility just rise in you. I brought herbs, and salt, and candles to bless the area."

To judge by my reactions, it didn't work. I walked around the clinic poking my nose into storage rooms, examination rooms, and offices. In the end storage room I felt dizzy. I didn't even want to enter the room labeled "Physician's Office." A couple of the examination rooms were fine, but in the largest treatment room, my heart started fluttering so much I couldn't get my breath—for me the sign of a strong presence.

I went back to the nurses' station and we began to talk. Bernadette, Patty, and Dr. Archer* were the most in control of the situation. Bernadette, with her dramatically flowing salt-and-pepper hair, sometimes channels in her non-nursing hours. There was Patty, the delightfully humorous earth-mother, given to exotic jewelry and herbal remedies. And Carol, a nervous, feathery-haired young woman who seemed on the verge of tears throughout our interview. Dr. Jack Archer, the man who first started the clinic, had a very calm, low-key, immensely reassuring manner.

It began in March, 1992; the clinic had only been in the building for about three months. All the patients were gone. Carol and Bernadette were chatting in the nurse's station when they saw the shadow of a man wearing a tall hat in the doctor's office. Thinking that there was a patient still in the office, they hushed. Then they realized that they could see the light in the office through the figure, yet it cast a shadow in the room as it walked.

Carol and Patty began to keep lists of the dates and times of manifestations, feeling slightly nuts for doing it.

"It was all such crazy stuff!" said Carol. "I could smell a man behind me, that sweat smell. It would stay with me for about a month, then disappear for a while. The printer kept turning off even though you can't bump the switch—it's under the copier. You'd go away and the copier would be turned off again. And it took ten minutes to heat up! After a while I wouldn't stay in the office alone."

Bernadette believed that the ghost singled out Carol, possibly because Carol had fewer psychic defenses. Bernadette is highly psychic, Patty and Dr. Archer have lived with ghosts.

Early one morning, before the clinic was open, Carol was filling the coffee pot in Room 4 when she heard a woman crying in the hallway.

"I was on the curb when Bernadette pulled up."

Doors kept getting locked or unlocked mysteriously. Everyone complained to the housekeeping staff who indignantly denied having anything to do with the doors, but admitted hearing the same noises. The nursing staff finally taped over the locks. Doors still locked themselves.

Carol heard the man in the hat flying down the hall by the nurses' station. "They were strong steps, brisk—like he was in a hurry."

But the horror did not always walk as a man. When Carol was working alone something shuffled by the nurse's station. Something on all fours that came pattering out of the treatment room area snuffling and dragging its paws like a huge animal.

"We called it the beast," Carol shuddered, "I just dropped the coffee pot and took off."

"Didn't you get a look at it?" I asked.

"Are you kidding!" Carol exclaimed, "It was bad enough hearing it!"

There was an inexplicable amount of rage in the office.

"I've never worked around so much conflict —over nothing," Dr. Archer told me. "One doctor, Dr. Lynne* got sick every time he came in. His blood pressure shot off the meter. He was relatively normal before he came to work here, then he began turning his back on patients, never looking at them while he took notes. He started wearing a surgical mask, then a respirator on his rounds. He now sells Amway."

Soon, even patients noticed the weirdness.

Bernadette was helping the last patient of the day with the hydrotub when they both saw the shadowy man with the hat on the wall.

"I'd locked up the inside and the outside doors. There was no one in the office except this patient and I. He looked at me and I looked at him, wondering how he would respond. He said, 'You have ghosts don't you?' 'Yes, we do,' I answered. 'He's a tall man with a hat on?' 'That's one of them.' 'Did you just see what I saw?' 'Yes, David, I did.'

"The paper on the examination table in the treatment room would be depressed as if someone were sitting there," Dr. Archer told me. "Judging from the size and weight, it was a man of about 160-180 pounds."

"We'd sit here out at the nurse's station and listen to the rolls of paper unroll and re-roll. You can't say anything to the patients because you work in a doctor's office," Carol said.

"The treatment room is where I felt the strongest presence," I said. The women exchanged glances.

"Where?" they asked eagerly, "Exactly where in the treatment room did you feel it?"

"I'm not really sure," I said, suddenly feeling a bit stupefied. "Let me walk back through it and I'll let you know." I went in the far door and walked by the curtain room divider. There I stopped. I stretched out my hands, palms down.

"It was right *here*," I said, patting the air for emphasis. As I did, I was submerged to the elbows in what felt like live electrical current. For a moment I was stunned. It was like putting my hands in a tub of water with a plugged-in hairdryer.

"Oh, my God," I said "I'm in it!"

My mind was racing. One part said, "This is crazy!" The other half stupidly said, "This is interesting! Let's see where this goes."

So instead of pulling my hands back, I kept them in the current. It was hot, wet, and painful. As I stood there, the heat and the current increased as if an unseen someone had their hand on the knob, turning up the voltage. When I couldn't stand it anymore, I yanked my hands out. I rushed away from the hot spot into the hall. Since I couldn't concentrate at the nurses' station, we moved into the waiting room to talk about the Treatment Room from Hell.

One patient, known as "Big Ed*" for his solid 400 pounds was sitting on a special "leg-lift" chair with his legs in a whirlpool tub. Bernadette was standing by, directing his leg into the water, when suddenly the chair began to vibrate and Big Ed started to fall forward on top of her. If she hadn't dodged, he would have crushed her to death in the tub. "We would have needed the Jaws of Life to get him off of me," she said wryly.

Mysteriously, machines malfunctioned whenever they were brought into the treatment room. Unusual breakdowns would occur: Three successive whirlpool baths began pumping oil against a gradient. Or pumping oil instead of water—something the manufacturer says is impossible.

As we sat in the waiting room, I felt a vibration going through my middle. Dr. Archer nodded.

"It's coming from over here," he pointed to the far corner of the building, the room labeled "Physician's Office" [the room I didn't want to enter] "I can feel it on this side of my head. There is a constant low-level vibration and a very high-pitched hum."

The vibration could explain why well-trained dogs misbehaved in the office or why, as Bernadette said, "People get more agitated here. There are 'hot spots' in the waiting room. We tried to keep people from sitting in them. One patient was a drug addict on methadone. Her sister, a paranoid schizophrenic, would drive her to her appointments. The addict kept talking about a dark force, moving like a big black blob through the waiting room, moving through the walls. We just chalked it up to her drug problem. Then her sister saw balls of light glowing in front of her. She got agitated and would not sit in the one hot spot that was empty."

The atmosphere affected the healthy staff too. Carol was a bundle of nerves. Patty, a normally happy, jovial woman, barely smiled.

As we talked, there came a single knock from under our feet. Patty said nonchalantly, "Oh, that's just under the floor."

"You mean that there are pipes under the floor that make noises?" I asked.

"No, the building is built on a cement slab. I mean it's *under* the floor."

I shuddered at the thought of something crawling around in the darkness below.

"In late August, 1992, we had to evacuate the building," Dr. Archer said. "It smelled like sewer gas in the office. The fire department came and found lethal levels of methane gas, with particularly high concentrations in the treatment room. They had no explanation." The waiting room still smells like mud.

The land used to be owned by a local industry. It has been documented that there is toxic waste buried on the property, "but the EPA has assured the landlord that it is safely buried," Patty added. Bernadette and Dr. Archer wondered if the ghosts were trying to drive them out of an unhealthy environment.

I left the clinic wondering if the staff needed an exorcist or the EPA.

Malevolent ghosts or toxic nightmares? The Clinic has changed hands, so only the future will tell. But Bernadette summed it up, "It was a place where the Dark Force was amplified. It was pure craziness all the time."

HIGHWAYS TO HELL
Haunted roads and bridges

Now he goes along the darksome road,
thither whence they say no one returns.
-Catallus-

Every county has one: a Spook Hollow, a Screaming-Mimi or Cry-baby Bridge (see "From the Cradle to the Grave" in Haunted Ohio II). It is the place you take your girl to scare up a little affection with tales of Hook Man or the Melonheads. It's the bridge where the baby cries or the woman screams at midnight, the road less traveled....

Here is an atlas of haunted highways that lead—no-where....

THE I-71 HITCHHIKER

Rich Heileman stared at the highway stretching out in front of him. It was nearly 1 a.m. Monday morning and he still had a half hour before he'd reach his home in Berea. There were no lights on this stretch of I-71, north of Medina, but way ahead he saw something pale on the right shoulder. It looked like a person wearing a light-colored coat, walking along the berm.

There was no other traffic on the freeway. "What's somebody doing out walking this time of night?" he thought to himself. "And I don't recall seeing any cars broken down along the side of the road. Maybe I'm just imagining this."

But as he got closer, the person was still there, a fairly young man, in his thirties, to judge by his posture and walk, with dark hair and a light tan raincoat.

Rich got really nervous. "What should I do? Maybe this guy needs a ride." All kinds of things went through his mind—picking up strange people late at night was dangerous, but he still wanted to help someone in trouble.

"I've got to make a decision," Rich thought, "I'll bet he's going to try to hitch."

Rich got within 300 feet, maybe closer. His headlights picked up the man who started to turn and put out his thumb.

"I never saw his face. Where his head was seemed to be dark, blanked out. I was real close to him when the headlights went through him. He looked suddenly transparent all over. I could still see him. Then he faded and was gone.

"My mind was racing over and over: 'Geez! What was that?! Did I imagine the whole thing? What the heck's going on?' Then I started thinking. 'Yeah, you did see it.' I saw the figure for too long a time. It gave me the creeps. I floored it all the way back to Berea. Seventy miles per hour was the top speed my little '65 VW Bug would do. I kept wishing I could go faster. It wasn't hallucination, I hadn't been drinking or ingesting other things. I wasn't overtired; I'm kind of a night owl anyway and 1:30 isn't that late for me. I was just concentrating on getting back home.

"I was really going through this thing in my mind: 'Should I stop? Nobody would be walking out there if they didn't need help. What am I going to do?' He solved the problem for me by disappearing. Then I had something else to think about...."

The next day, Rich, a Cleveland-area newspaper reporter, met his friend Mitch for lunch.

"You're never going to guess what happened. I was driving home from Medina to Berea on I-71. I saw...."

Mitch stopped him in mid-sentence: "Don't tell me. You saw the I-71 hitchhiker." And he told Rich that the police and sheriff have had many reports about the vanishing man.

"I've driven that route since, any number of times, but I've never seen anything again. Maybe you have to be there at the right time."

Or it could be that you have to be in just the right frame of mind. Rich was concentrating on getting home. Maybe the hitchhiker was too.

THE MAN WITHOUT A FACE

Champaign County is a place where the past and present meet as companionably as neighboring farmers discussing the weather over a fence.

"That's the thing I notice about living here: The continuity of history," said Nina*. "The farm next door has been owned by the same family for 150 years. My neighbors speak of the man who built the house across the road 100 years ago as if he were still alive."

Sitting in the sunny kitchen of her 150-year old house, Nina talked of local history and legend.

"Just out back here," she gestured towards the deck, "there used to be an enormous honey-locust tree. It's gone now, but we still have honey-locust saplings all over the yard that must have come from that same tree."

She pointed to a small stream running along the property.

"That's King's Creek. It was named after a Shawnee general whom Logan's men called 'His Royal Highness.' We don't know his real name. Logan's men weren't sure if he was really a high chief, but he wore better clothes and more ornaments than the other warriors so they assumed he was a king."

As Logan's men marched through what was then a prairie fen, "His Royal Highness" hid in the long grass until the last soldier had passed, then rose out of the weeds and fired. His gun misfired, giving the soldier time to raise his musket, and blow the Shawnee's face off.

After this, legend had it that if you took the path by the honey-locust tree at dark, "His Royal Highness" would be waiting for you up in its branches, blood dripping from his ruined clot of a face. He would howl and scream until you were almost mad with fear. It got so that travelers would detour miles out of their way to avoid the honey-locust tree.

"It's a good legend," said Nina "it really sounds like a ghost—or an owl."

I agreed. With their flat or scooped-out faces, an owl might look very like a man with his face blown off to a panicked traveler in the dark.

Nina got out a bird book. She pointed out various types of owls she had seen on their property. There it was: the common screech owl in its rufous (or red) phase. No other owl has such bright red feathers. Owls are immensely territorial and sometimes attack people they perceive as a threat. "And they sound like someone being knifed," added Nina.

The early settlers lived and traveled in a world with no electricity and no street lights. The woods were teeming with wildlife. Their barns and outbuildings were filled with owls. Surely they would have recognized an owl when they heard it? Or were they just an ignorant superstitious lot, afraid of their own shadows?

Common screech owl or bloody-faced Indian chief? Only time could have told.

THE HAUNTED HANDS

Back in the 1860s, in what is now Pike Lake Park, a group of settlers had gathered for a community log-burning. By nightfall so many log fires were burning that the cleared area was as bright as day. The jug was passed, the fiddler fiddled like the very devil himself, and more logs were heaped on the huge fires. Everyone took turns poking the logs to keep them burning quickly. There was much laughter as the sparks shot into the night sky like fireworks or showered down on the workers.

One young woman in a red plaid shawl took a pole and worked together with the young men, her cheeks glowing scarlet. Someone called her name and she turned, still holding her pole to the blaze. Suddenly the huge pile of logs shifted and rolled over onto her.

Everyone scattered, and when they looked back, swatting

the cinders from their eyes, the young woman in the red shawl
lay screaming, her hands trapped beneath a pile of burning
logs. By the time the men heaved the logs off her arms, she
was unconscious. Everyone gasped at the horror that lay there,
for the hardwood had burnt white-hot.

The doctor shook his head when he saw the blackened
stubs of charred bone. He asked someone to boil oil. The wrist
stumps would have to be cauterized after he amputated. He cut
off the young woman's hands halfway between wrist and
elbow. Holding his breath against the stink, his assistant
carried the hands into the forest and dropped them into a rotten
tree stump. By the time he returned, the doctor was wiping his
saw on a rag and repacking it in his bag. Weeping women
covered the young woman's sooty, distorted face.

After that, horses shied and reared as their riders passed
the rotten stump. As the horses ran, nostrils flaring, a stench
floated after them—something like burnt sausages.

Other travelers, riding watchfully through the forest at
night reported being clutched at the throat or knees by an
invisible attacker. When they tried to seize the arms of the
ghostly strangler, they grasped only air. Others claimed that
when they walked through the darkened forest, a cold hand,
smelling of burning flesh, slipped into theirs. Some scoffed at
the witnesses but they still avoided the forest path.

Travelers today would do well to do the same. Pike Lake
Park is still said to be haunted by a pair of disembodied hands
that grab at ankle or neck—blackened hands that twitch their
way through the forest like charred spiders.[1]

DEATH WISH

It was about 9:30 on a warm night in 1982. Carol
Harbaugh was driving south on Plum Street in Springfield. She
had just passed Fern Cliff Cemetery, crossed over the creek
that runs through Snyder Park, and was on her way up the hill
when a man walked into her headlights.

"He walked from the driver's side diagonally into my
lights. He seemed to be slightly built, about five foot, eight

inches, even though I couldn't see the top part of him because it was in darkness. He wore rumpled grey work trousers and black work shoes. He took two or three steps into the headlights. I took my foot off the accelerator to brake—and he disappeared.

"I thought he was just jaywalking. I got this intense tingly sensation I get in my wrists when I'm terribly frightened. I knew there was no way I could avoid hitting him; he was walking right into the car!"

Lemoine Rice, a psychic researcher who leads the class in psychic phenomena and development where I met Carol, had a similar story to tell.

He was driving towards Columbus on Rt. 40 a little past the old TB Sanitarium about 9:00 p.m. in mid-October 1973.

"I was going about 50 mph when all of a sudden, this guy walked right in front of my car out of the median strip. I swerved into the left lane to miss him without even looking to see if another car was behind me. When I looked in my rearview mirror, he wasn't there. I was so shaken up, I had to pull off the road. Then I turned the car around and tried to find him. There was no one there.

"He was a caucasian male, about thirty years old, maybe six foot, lanky. He was wearing dark clothes and he took very long steps, almost as if he were running. I got the idea he was trying to throw himself in front of my car. But why would somebody walk into your car?—unless they had a death wish...." he left the thought hanging.

THE SNOW CHILD

It was a dark, snowy winter's morning. About 5 a.m. Charles Flick was running Rt. 163 E out of Oak Harbor on his way to work. The land is flat there and in winter the snow sweeps across it, leaving a moonscape of drifts. Flick had just passed the business district. A few houses lined the road, then snow-blurred fields. It had snowed hard that night and the road hadn't yet been plowed.

Suddenly, just in the reach of his headlights, Flick saw a figure in the road. "It was a kid," he recalls, "about age thirteen or fourteen. A chunky kid. He looked right at me." The figure was wearing dark pants, a dark coat and boots and a stocking cap with a white band.

"I thought maybe somebody's car had broken down and the kid was signaling for help. I glanced away from the boy, just for a minute, to look for a car. When I looked back, he was gone. I kept thinking, 'Did I see it?'"

This rattled Flick so much he stopped the car and walked back to the approximate spot where he had seen the young boy. The road was snow-covered. There were no signs of any car but Flick's and no footprints.

THE HIGH-LEVEL HAUNT

Alan, a Cleveland man who is very sensitive to spirits, told me the following story:

In my hometown of Lorain, there is a long, arching bridge that passes over the Black River. In August, 1982 about 11:00 p.m. I was headed to the East Side on a ten-speed. The bridge was a favorite place to ride because of the speeds you could reach coming down off the steep bridge. I was doing about 40 mph when I came off the end and onto the sidewalk.

I'd just hit the curve, when, about fifteen yards ahead of me, I saw a young woman. She looked to be in her early twenties, quite attractive, slim, with shoulder-length blonde hair. She wore an open-collar white shirt, blue jeans, and white deck shoes. She was just standing there running one hand through her hair. The area was well-lit and she looked solid and real.

The sidewalk was very narrow and there was no way I could maneuver around her, so I yelled a warning, yanking on both brake levers, hoping I could stop in time.

Suddenly, she was gone. I brought the bike to a complete stop a few feet past where she'd been standing and looked around, but I couldn't see her. Had she stepped over the curb and crossed the highway? I should have been able to see her crossing the road. If she had gone towards the river, I would have heard her crunching through the dry grass and weeds. She just plain wasn't there.

I slowly scooted the bike along with my feet, trying to figure out how she'd vanished that fast. Then I saw something that gave me a chill. About ten yards beyond where she had stood, there was a chuckhole right in the middle of the sidewalk. If I had hit the hole, I probably would have lost control of the bike and either fallen or been thrown across the curb into the road.

Was she a real person? Was she a guardian angel? I've lived in Lorain most of my life and I know just about every haunted spot in the area, but I've never heard of the High-Level Bridge being haunted.

GONNA RIDE THAT TRAIN

Edward Giles and Sam Austin had time to kill when they found themselves between trains at Huntington, West Virginia. Ed had heard of the amazing powers of Mrs. Saidie Blake of Chesapeake and proposed that they give her a try.

"I'll go along," said Sam, "but I don't believe in that stuff about calling up the dead."

They argued the point until they were near the Ohio ferry landing. Then Sam said, "I'll prove my point by sitting here on the track until you get back. Tell the old lady you want to talk to your friend, Sam Austin. Then when a voice answers, you'll know what a fake she really is."

"All right," Ed said, "I'll take you up on that. Maybe we'll both learn something."

It took Ed nearly an hour to cross the river and locate the medium's house in Chesapeake. She happened to be free and immediately agreed to contact Ed's friend.

Holding a long tin horn in his lap, Ed watched the woman drop into a trance. Then a voice he instantly recognized said from the horn, "Well, Ed, I am actually here,"

"Sure you are!" said Ed, "You're sitting across there on the railroad tracks."

"No." said the voice, "While watching the ferry cross the river I must have dozed off. I never even heard the train that struck and killed me. I learned a lesson about life after death, all right, but what a price!"

The voice died away and the medium came out of her trance asking what had come through.

Ed told her, adding curtly, "That just goes to show that you don't know what you are talking about. My friend is very much alive, sitting across the river waiting on me."

"I wouldn't say that," said Mrs. Blake wearily.

Ed left the house swearing he'd never be taken in again by a fake medium. Talking to the dead—it was all bunk!

As he boarded the ferry, he saw a large crowd on the other side of the river. "What's going on?" he asked the steward.

"Some fellow went to sleep on the railroad track and a train ran over him."

"Did it kill him?"

"Instantly. He's been taken to the Huntington morgue until someone can identify him."

Ed hurried to the morgue and asked to see the train victim. When the sheet was pulled back, there was Sam's body, smiling peacefully.[2]

THE INDIAN IN THE ROAD

R.J. Abraham is a native Athenian, who teaches a course on "Haunted Athens." He lives in the oldest house in Athens, built in 1816 and shared this story:

"I saw 'Tecumseh' on the hill standing on one of the two Indian mounds on my property. One summer, my yard-boy came running down the hill as the lawn-mower roared away in the other direction. I thought he'd been stung by a bee or wasp, but he said he thought he had seen an Indian—standing in exactly the same spot where I had seen him two summers before.

"Another summer, a friend of mine was using the pool when she called that she 'saw' an Indian on the same hill. Ironically, she was performing in the outdoor theatre production of *Tecumseh* that summer. She became very nervous and said she had a premonition that something dreadful was going to happen.

"Within the hour, a car came speeding down a steep hill near my house. It continued across the highway, passing between two cars—each coming from opposite directions—and crashed into a building. The driver walked away without a scratch. He explained that his brakes had failed, but he felt as if someone had taken the wheel and timed the passing between the two cars, guiding him to his safe crash-landing. I didn't know Indians knew how to drive!"

BLOODY BRIDGE

The bridge is now covered with aluminum paint, but that hasn't erased its name—"Bloody Bridge"—or the tragedy that gave the bridge that name. Walk across the bridge when the moon is full and you might see the ghostly face of Minnie Warren floating like the moon in the dark waters.

Bloody Bridge spans the Miami-Erie Canal seven miles south of the Allen County town of Spencerville on Rt. 66. It has been rebuilt several times since the 1850s, when the tragedy occurred, but the legend remains.

Two mule drivers named Bill and Jack whose teams pulled boats along the canal, both fell in love with Minnie, the daughter of a canal boat captain. Minnie was flattered by their attentions, but she only had eyes for Jack. If the two rivals happened to pass, Bill and Jack would sing out friendly greetings—Bill through teeth clenched in hatred.

One evening, while the boats were being unloaded, Jack and Minnie attended a party to which Bill had conspicuously not been invited. With his singlemindedness about Minnie and his rage at Jack, Bill wasn't a popular guest. The party ended early the next morning and Jack escorted Minnie back to her father's boat.

As the couple came to the bridge, Bill leaped from behind an abutment, an ax in his hands. With one blow, he severed the head of his rival. Twitching and flopping, the body slumped to the road while the blood fountained from the arteries. Minnie had time to scream only once before the ax descended and her head splashed into the river.

Bill disappeared until, many years later, a skeleton and a rusted ax head were found in a nearby well.

The sweethearts' blood stained the bridge so deeply that traces of it could be seen for twenty years afterward. When the old bridge was razed in 1904, souvenir hunters tore it to pieces. And until the 1940s, the new Bloody Bridge was, appropriately, painted red.[3]

A GHOST'S HOME IS HIS CASTLE
Franklin Castle and others

While from a proud tower in the town
Death looks gigantically down.
-Edgar Allan Poe-

Ohio is not a place you would expect to find an abundance of castles, let alone haunted ones. But Ohio, the haunt of it all, continues to surprise....

SQUIRE'S CASTLE

In the 1890s Feargus Bowden Squire and his daughter visited the Chagrin Valley and were enchanted with its beauty. Squire purchased 525 acres about 16 miles east of Cleveland where he planned to build a country estate like those of his native England. A prominent New York architect designed two structures in a romantic combination of the English Tudor and German baronial style: a gatekeeper's lodge and a mansion to be built overlooking the Chagrin Valley.

The gatekeeper's lodge was built first of stone quarried on the property, a miniature image of what the main building was to be with its rugged stone exterior, half-timbering, a crenellated tower—even crenellated chimneys. The Squire family used the lodge for their country "cottage," occupied on weekends and for weeks during the summer.

But Squire's country mansion was never built and in 1922 Squire sold the estate to a syndicate who sold it to the Metropolitan Park Board in 1925. The Board made the land the nucleus of the North Chagrin Reservation and "Squire's Castle" as the gatekeeper's lodge became known, was turned into a picnic shelter.

Naturally, romantic—and haunting—legends have grown up around the miniature castle. One says that plans for the proposed mansion were abandoned when Squire's wife, Louisa died. Mr. Squire, utterly heartbroken, could not face building the dream house they were to have shared. It's a romantic story, but Mrs. Squire died in 1927—five years after the property was sold. Mr. Squire died in 1932.

But every castle needs a ghost story and Squire's Castle is reputed to be haunted by the ghost of Louisa Squire. Although Mr. Squire enjoyed his country castle and spent summers there with his daughter and the caretakers, Mrs. Squire despised the isolation of the castle. She came for visits, but she hated the jolting trip down dusty dirt roads, and claimed that she was awakened at night by the screams of wild animals, for the northern woods still harbored panthers.

The tale goes that a terrified Louisa would wander throughout the castle with a red lantern to light her way. One night she blundered into the room where her husband displayed his hunting trophies. The heads leering down on her in the dark, their long teeth stained with the dim red light, unhinged her mind. Running through the castle she caught her head on a rope on the steps to the basement and hung herself. You can still see her red lantern bobbing through the windows.

Yet another rumor had it that Mrs. Squire was insane. She actually led a very active social life, contributing much time to charities, especially the Red Cross. But mysteriously, her social life came to an abrupt end several years before her death. Mr. Squire was quoted as saying this was "due to a fall."

Ghost hunter Robert Van Der Velde suggests that the story about Mrs. Squire's basement hanging was at least partially true. Perhaps the socialite was incapacitated, either deliberately or by accident, turning her into a recluse and making her restless soul wander about the site.

The Castle stands on a knoll a thousand feet from the road.

For many years it was used as a picnic shelter, but vandals destroyed the interior, leaving only a stone shell. Several years ago the upper floors were removed and the windows and doors were bricked up. As a final mysterious touch, the basement was filled with cement, leaving two overgrown steps that lead nowhere. Whatever secret Mrs. Squire encountered on the basement steps has been sealed up for eternity.[1]

CHATEAU LAROCHE

When I was young, I was enchanted by a photo of "Chateau Laroche in the grip of winter" showing a Frank Lloyd Wright vision of a castle. I found the reality to be somewhat smaller and shabbier.

It was pouring rain when Katy and I arrived. Wisps of straw spread over the muddy walk didn't do much good. Several burly men in CAT hats snickered together in the entrance hall.

Inside it was much smaller than I expected. There was no hammerbeamed great hall, but a series of rooms small enough to be heated by fireplace, and floors linked by cramped spiral staircases with irregular steps. A bedroom and kitchen occupied circular corner chambers.

The floor was powdered with rock dust and yet at the same time damp. Dead flies lay at the bottom of the smeary glass display case. Bare bulbs scarcely lit the tiny rooms. A hand-lettered sign advertised a raffle to win the chance to spend the night at the castle. I noticed motion detectors in every room. What is the caretaker afraid will creep through these rooms at night?

The chapel was a cramped little oblong room with the Ten Commandments, crudely carved and out of order, on cement plaques. One alcove seemed meant for an altar. A few small stained glass windows set in arrow slits overlooked the river. It was a claustrophobic room, made more so by the smell. Katy and I noticed it at the same time: sweet and smoky, like cannabis or incense or dead flowers. The smell hung only in the chapel.

This crusaders' castle in miniature was built the old-fashioned way with stones and mortar and muscle, practically singlehandedly by Harry D. Andrews over a span of 51 years. Who was this man? What drove him to try to build Camelot on the banks of the Little Miami?

Andrews was born in New York state in 1890 and studied architecture all over the world. During World War I, Andrews served in the medical corps and the intelligence division. He fell in love with French castles and stayed on in France after the war, studying Norman architecture at Toulouse University.

Returning to the United States, Andrews settled in Cleveland. There he taught Sunday school classes and in 1927 he bought some land near Loveland where his young men's class could camp. When their tents wore out, two small stone rooms were built, which can still be seen at the base of the towers facing the river.

During the Great Depression, some of his workers left for the Civilian Conservation Corps during the Great Depression. Andrews took in several homeless boys and work continued. In the 1950s, Andrews turned his attention entirely to the castle. Supplies had to be sledded down a hill in back because the road to the castle hadn't yet been built.

In 1955 Andrews moved into the Dome Room, a round room with an unusual stone dome that experts said couldn't be built. The only heat came from a wood-burning fireplace. Andrews also constructed a dungeon with two cells and thirty-inch walls—used as the neighborhood bomb shelter in the nervous days of nuclear preparedness.

The sheer statistics of the structure are mind-boggling:

Andrews personally carried some four thousand pailsful of stone to lay the road's foundation. The main entrance door is made of 233 pieces of wood studded with more than 2,500 nails—protection against berserkers' axes. Andrews lined his 80-foot well in the courtyard north of the castle with bricks made by filling some 32,000 quart-size milk cartons with concrete. The floors are insulated against damp by 14-inch-thick concrete poured over 1,000 quart oil cans. A 220-foot retaining wall, 10 feet high and 2 feet thick, said to contain more stones than the entire castle, keeps the whole thing from sliding into the river.

Throughout the castle hang photos, newspaper articles, and mementos of Andrews: his high school yearbook, religious poems written under the pen name Harry N. Drews, a newsletter open to a page where Andrews answers a young knight's query: "Is it OK for a knight to have a girl-friend?" One photo shows Andrews smiling into the sun on the roof of the castle. He is a good-looking man with grey hair and rimless glasses, a strong jaw and nose. There are also hundreds of photos of the young men who have joined "Sir Harry's" knightly order: The Knights of the Golden Trail, modern Knights Templar, whose teen-age pages and squires promise to uphold the Ten Commandments and who even now continue to build. Andrews died in 1981 from burns suffered in a trash fire.

Up on the roof, the rain stood in puddles. I got a sense of what it might have been like to stand watch on a tower in the rain, chain mail rusting. Inside I felt the twilight lives of medieval castle dwellers: light filtering through arrow slits and smoke from the fireplaces making the eyes smart. There was nothing noble about life in a castle—it was a damp, dark, and dirty existence.

I, for one, would not be eager to spend the night here. There was something unwholesome about the atmosphere. Perhaps it was the damp, the decaying smell from the river. Perhaps it was the confidential sound of the men in CAT hats talking among themselves.

"Have you seen the dungeon?" one of them asked. The others guffawed. Katy and I politely walked over to a stair that spiraled down into darkness. We looked at it, then at each other.

"I'm *not* going down there," Katy said firmly.

"Wimp," I murmured.

[Later, in the car, we found that we had the identical thought: The men were planning to lock us in the dungeon—just for fun, of course, eventually letting us out.]

"Any ghost stories?" I asked the men, turning back from
the stairs. They took the question seriously.

"Sir Harry supposedly hangs around here," said one, his
forehead furrowed. "Oh, and there's a mysterious smell, but
only in the chapel...."

The next time Katy and I visited, it was a sunny spring
day. Flowers bloomed in the beds. Knights of the Golden
Trail were working on the terraced gardens. I asked the
younger man in the CAT hat at the desk if there were any ghost
stories. He grinned. "Nah. Unless you count the time we had
wall-to-wall Cub Scouts sleeping here overnight. In the
morning they found all their shoes knotted together by the
strings."

The atmosphere, with windows and doors open, and the
energy of other visitors, was less oppressive. Shiny steel
blades gleamed in a new display case. The chapel boasted a
new carved wooden throne. This time we descended into the
dungeon with a group of children. The smooth cement walls
and floor were well-scrubbed and swept, their curves organic,
like the belly of a living creature.

Behind a wooden grill sat a chair in a tiny room, surrounded by hundreds of bottles. I thought of prisoners walled
up to starve. At the end of the dungeon was a cell with a glass
door. The children stood on a box to see a manacled skeleton
among the canning jars, lit by a lurid red light.

As we walked back to the car, I wondered what obsession
had driven Andrews. A publicity brochure states: "Chateau
Laroche was built as an expression and reminder of the simple
strength and rugged grandeur of the mighty men who lived
when Knighthood was in flower. It was their knightly zeal for
honor, valor and manly purity that lifted mankind out of the
moral midnight of the dark ages, and started it towards a gray
dawn of human hope."

I noticed a round window hidden in shadow. I peered in.
As my eyes adjusted to the gloom, I could see a stone alcove
containing a red plaid shirt like Andrews had worn in so many

of his pictures, and milk carton molds for cement blocks. It was like a reliquary, a shrine to this man who built his monument in stone.[2]

FRANKENSTEIN'S CASTLE

The Stone Tower, Patterson Tower, Witches' Tower, Frankenstein's Castle—whatever name you call it, it is a startling sight: A Norman keep overlooking Dayton's Community Golf Course along Patterson Avenue. There are no records of when or why it was built. Researchers studying Hills and Dales Park, suggest that it was built by CWA workers in the 1930s as an observation tower. Others believe John D. Patterson built it.

In the 1960s, a group of teenagers were hanging out at the tower when a summer thunderstorm blew in. They scrambled inside and sat on the stairs, laughing and talking, confident that they were safe. After all, the walls were nearly a foot thick. But lightning struck the tower, and sizzled down the metal stair rail, electrocuting two of the teens. For weeks you could see scorch marks on the walls. After that, metal plates were riveted over the door and over the barred slit windows.

Now, on thunderous nights, it is said, you can see the black silhouettes of the two dead teenagers suddenly light up as lightning explodes at the tower.

The metal plates covering the upper windows have been wrenched off by the curious so that you can see the bars at the windows, the spiral staircase leading to the top of the tower. The ground in front of the tower's door is scorched in a spidery pattern. Another lightning strike? Bonfires set by kids just hanging out? Or an eternal reminder of a fiery tragedy?

THE SUNBATHING SPIRIT OF SCHWARZ CASTLE

Schwarz Castle stands like a watchtower on the Rhine, its five-story tower dominating the Third Street entrance to German Village. The Castle was built in the mid-1800s by Frederick William Schwarz, a wealthy German immigrant. He owned an apothecary shop on Main Street and nothing but the best was good enough for his bride-to-be, who remained in Germany while the house was being built. When the mansion was almost finished, Schwarz got a 'Dear Frederick' letter from his fiancee.

After that Schwarz turned eccentric and reclusive, adding secret rooms and passageways, including five levels of basement to the Castle. Sharing the Castle with his two unmarried sisters and his widowed mother, he became a vegetarian, drank only rainwater, let his hair grow long, wore only wool next to his skin, jogged around the block in his bare feet 365 days a year, and sunbathed nude on top of the turret. Through the window of the tower, the ladder he climbed is still visible.

Reportedly a man hung himself in one of the basements. After the castle was turned into apartments in the 1970s, two brothers argued over whether one of them was too drunk to drive. The drunken brother stabbed the other to death in a second-floor apartment. Some say you can still hear them quarreling.

Schwarz himself died in 1914, and it has been reported that his ghost can be seen looking out of a second-floor window or, white hair flying in the wind, climbing the ladder to the tower where he still sunbathes—the naked and the dead.[3]

THE HAUNTING OF FRANKLIN CASTLE

It *looks* like a haunted house: massive, dark, stone-block walls, a turret, several balconies, a 4-foot iron fence, and a kind of brooding presence. The story of Franklin Castle has everything: sex, murder, moans in the night, human bones walled up in a secret passageway—and ghosts.

This Cleveland landmark has been a clubhouse for German singing societies and a German socialist organization. It has been a doctor's office, private apartments, a party house, and, some say, a bootleggers' establishment. No one ever stayed for long....

Some former residents will tell you that the house has a life of its own or that it feeds on the lives of those who inhabit it. It is a house hard to walk away from, yet it has claimed a part of everyone who ever lived there. Some wonder if the house is a living entity, its windows the multiple eyes of a spider, its wrought-iron balconies like entrapping webs, its doors opening like venomous jaws. But is it an evil house or merely a sad one?

The bare bones of the story are these:

Hannes Tiedemann was born in Germany in 1833. In a contemporary photograph, he stands with his feet apart in a combative pose. He has a fierce, sand-colored beard, a mouth that turns down at one side, and narrow, suspicious eyes set in a troubled face.

His wife Luise wears a velvet dress with lace collar and cuffs. Her dark hair is parted in the middle over her lovely pre-Raphaelite face, with its high cheekbones and sad martyr's smile. Tiedemann does not look like an easy man to live with.

In Cincinnati he left his barrel-making business to join Weideman Co., a wholesale grocery and liquor concern. Eventually he went into banking—an enormous leap socially for the German tradesman immigrant. Newly rich, Tiedemann spared no expense in building this flamboyant Romanesque-revival mansion.

It boasts at least twenty-one rooms (the count varies), a fourth-floor ballroom reached by a spiral staircase, richly carved woodwork and marble fireplaces, wine cellars, dumb-waiters, and hidden passageways leading to secret rooms. Every inch of the house seems covered with ornament: even the interior shutters are fastened with hinges carved with birds and butterflies.

Hidden passages abound. At the rear of the house is a small room. Carefully hidden in the floor is a trap door leading to a tunnel that runs for some distance between the floor and the ceiling below. Then it stops.

A tiny circular staircase uncoils from the servants' hall to the foyer where the maid could emerge like an apparition from a hidden panel to answer the bell.

Another hidden room was said to contain a still, remnant of Prohibition. Yet another secret room was found to contain human bones: hundreds of babies—all butchered within recent times, said some. An inept doctor's botched patients, said others. Medical specimens, was another verdict. *Old* bones, said the Coroner.

Yet another secret room was the site of a mass murder—some twenty German socialists machine-gunned to death in a political dispute. Others say the secret room also contained a Nazi spy's radio and bales of Nazi propaganda literature. But this was much in the future...

Tiedemann married Luise; she bore a son, August, and a daughter, Emma. But in 1881 the family began its slide into tragedy. Fifteen-year old Emma died on January 16. The cause of death was listed as "diabetes," at that time a horrible lingering starvation for which there was no cure or relief. In April, the 84-year old matriarch, Wiebeka, died of "old age."

In the next two years, Luise and Hannes buried three babies, one just eleven days old. Overwhelmed by so many deaths, Luise decided to remodel the house, seeking distraction in noise and building, and, perhaps, bottles from those wine cellars.

On March 24, 1895, Luise died at the age of fifty-seven of what was recorded as "liver trouble." Her funeral was held in the front parlor of the house and the family coachmen carried her coffin to the hearse for the final drive to Riverside Cemetery.

Ever restless, Hannes made plans to build an even grander house on Lake Road. He sold the Franklin St. house to a brewer named Muhlhauser from Buffalo who sold the castle to the Socialist Eintracht Club in 1913. In a nostalgic mood, Tiedemann revisited a German resort where he and Luise had spent many summers. There he met (or perhaps re-met) a waitress named Henriette. Seeking immortality in her arms, he married the young woman in haste and repented at leisure. His will cut her off without a *pfenig*.

Then August died, aged 41, of a stroke. August's own two children both died before they were 40. The family died off, one by one, until only old Tiedemann was left. Hannes was stricken "suddenly while walking in the park," stated his obituary, concluding that the cause of death was a stroke. Others suggested he had been struck down by the hand of God for his sins.

It is difficult to separate legend from fact when dealing with the Castle. Legends tell of a bloody ax murder in the front tower room. Neighbors have long sworn that they see a woman in black staring down at them from the tower windows.

Surrounding the ballroom, with its 14-foot ceiling, are more hidden passageways. Legend says that in one of these Tiedemann hung his 13-year-old niece (or illegitimate daughter, Karen) from a rafter either because she was insane or promiscuous (which would have been considered insanity in a well-brought-up Victorian girl.) It was also whispered that he found the girl in bed with his grandson.

Still others say a young servant girl was murdered in the servant's quarters on her wedding day because she had rejected Tiedemann's advances. Another version points out a room where Tiedemann's mistress Rachel was tied up, gagged, and shot because she wanted to marry another man. It is said that you can hear her choking in the room. Perhaps it is her slight figure, dressed in black, that is sometimes seen on the balcony.

The stifled cries of an infant have been heard coming from the walls. There are mysterious electrical disturbances. Visitors have complained of seeing faces etched in the stone walls, nervousness, even of being overcome by some alien personality. Uneasy visitors have told me they heard mutterings in the walls.

One man who delivered papers at the Castle as a boy knocked at the door to collect. A woman's voice said, "Come in." As he stood in the front hall, a woman in filmy white drifted down the steps, and out through the closed front door.

Mr. and Mrs. James Romano and their children lived at the Castle for six fear-filled years. They originally bought the building to open a restaurant, but something always foiled their plans.

The day the Romanos moved in, the children, two sets of

twins age two and three, went upstairs to play. Later they came down and asked if they could take a cookie up to their friend, a little girl who was crying. Mrs. Romano thought they had invented an imaginary playmate, although the children insisted she was real. One daughter said, "Mommy, she dresses funny. She has real long dresses. And she talks kind of funny."

Mrs. Romano seemed the most affected by the house, believing that there were many spirits on the third floor. In a newspaper interview she said, "I'll tell you what I've done. They tell me I shouldn't have, that it's very dangerous; but I've sort of made a pact with what's here in this house...I spend a lot of time alone in this house and I would find myself walking from floor to floor and then suddenly I would...start crying for no reason...just cry as if my heart was going to break. And I didn't know why.

"They claim the original owner, Mrs. Tiedemann, is in this house and she possesses me. And at times I feel as if I'm not myself. It's very hard to explain but I feel that what I want to say doesn't come out. something else comes out, you see? [The priest] told me to go up and pray for her.

"The priest feels they are all evil. He feels I should get out of here because they'll affect me very badly. He said you can't trust them. But I said the spirits are very good to me, that are here. They've opened doors for me and everything. They've kept me from falling down the steps where others have been pushed down the steps. And he said they're very good to you until they get you in their grasp and then they become evil and make you do evil things."

When a psychic researcher visited with a medium, Mrs. Romano was inexplicably furious with the medium and nearly attacked her.

"I lived in fear, all that time they were here, that [the medium] was going to tell a secret. And there's a secret here in this house and I don't know what it is but I'm afraid somebody's going to find it. I feel I have to live there to protect this secret."

The Romanos sold the house in September of 1974 to Sam Muscatello who planned to make the structure a church. Instead he spent most of his time leading ghost-tours through the building and coping with ghostly manifestations. During his ownership, John Webster, a Cleveland radio executive, brought a tape recorder to the Castle for a radio special.

"I was climbing the stairs, with a large tape recorder strapped over my shoulder, when something that I couldn't see tore the recorder from my shoulders. I just stood there holding the microphone as I watched the tape-recorder flying down to the bottom of the stairs, where it broke into pieces."

Muscatello sold the house to a doctor, who sold the Castle to Michael DeVinko in 1979 for the same amount she paid for it.

But this is one ghost story with a happy ending. DeVinko has tried to restore the looming hulk of the house to its original beauty.

"Until I came into this, no one else did a thing," DeVinko said. "Maybe that's why I've had no problems here. I think that whatever or whoever may be here knows that I'm taking better care of this place than they thought."

DeVinko successfully tracked down the original blue-prints, which had been sold to a buyer in Nova Scotia, pieces of furniture that originally belonged to the house, and even the original house key, which still worked after several decades. DeVinko collected enough unusual coincidences to make one almost believe in reincarnation.

DeVinko estimated that he spent over $1.3 million restoring Franklin Castle, which, by his count has twenty-eight rooms and eighty windows. He had plans to restore the carriage house roof, the *port-cochere*, and the elevator, but in 1994 the house went on the market again.

Perhaps Hannes and Luise weren't building a house, but a legend. Perhaps houses, even haunted ones, need love too. And when Franklin Castle felt mistreated by uncaring tenants, perhaps it acted to get rid of them. Has the house, at last, come home?[4]

TALES FROM THE CRYPT
More ghosts in cemeteries

*I sing, as the Boy does by the
Burying Ground—because I am afraid.*
-Emily Dickinson-

Graveyards have always been rumored to be the haunt of spirits. In folklore, the spirit of the first person buried there becomes the graveyard guardian. In the barbaric past, a living person might be sacrificed in a new cemetery, to keep an eye-socket on things.

In my personal experience, graveyard ghosts are a rarity. People haunt where they lived, not necessarily where their bones are buried. Yet, there's something about a graveyard that conjures up our deepest-buried fears...

WHEN THE ROLL IS CALLED UP YONDER

The white marble tombstones stand like soldiers at ease under the tall trees in Johnson's Island Confederate Cemetery. It is a pleasant shady place on a summer's day, but it was hell on earth for some 10,000 Confederate prisoners during the Civil War. Dubbed "Uncle Sam's Confederate Hotel" by its inmates, the conditions at the prison camp were appalling. Diseases like dysentery and cholera raged unchecked. Barracks were poorly heated and blankets were withheld as retaliation for the supposed mistreatment of Union prisoners. Food was scanty and the starvation rations often included rat. Many soldiers died; 206 men were buried under wooden grave markers carved from bunk boards.

Just after the turn of the century the United Daughters of the Confederacy heard of the cemetery's poor condition and replaced the rotting wood markers with Georgia marble. In June 1910, the cemetery was dedicated with the unveiling of a bronze statue of a Confederate soldier. In 1915 a group of 150 Italian laborers were working a small quarry on the island. They lived in flimsy shacks, quarrying limestone to build breakwaters at Cleveland, Lorain and Cedar Point.

That March a fierce thunderstorm swept in off the water. The men fled to the ruined remains of some prison buildings near the cemetery to escape the lightening and wind. As the thunder roared like cannon, the terrified men saw the statue of the Confederate soldier turn slowly on its pedestal and face the 206 graves.

The statue raised its bronze bugle and blew reveille. As the Italians watched in horror, a glowing mist began to rise from the ground. It wavered, then took on the form of men in grey uniforms, their hollow-eyed faces the ghastly phosphorescent green of something that has rotted underground for a long time.

The lightning slashed like a sword through the clouds. The soldiers stood at attention, then each man shouldered his rifle. And the ghostly company marched off into oblivion.[1]

THE UNLUCKY HORSESHOE

James K. Henry of Perry County just couldn't decide. He had a mind to get married, but the question was, which of the two girls he had been courting—Rachel Hodge or Mary Angle—to marry? They were both attractive and they were both willing—that was the trouble. Perplexed, he harnessed up his favorite horse, Bob, and went for a buggy ride to sort things out. Rachel was the better cook, but Mary loved to ride and she was fun to squeeze at a dance. Rachel was pretty and quiet, but there was something in her eyes... Henry turned the matter over and over in his mind until he dozed off from the sheer effort of so much thinking.

He started awake as Bob sneezed. The buggy had stopped at the gate of Mary Angle's home. James's spirits rose. Surely it was fate that the decision had been made for him. He gave the horse a pat, then confidently he strode up to the door and asked to speak to Mary's father.

Mary and James were married in 1844. Rachel Hodge was one of the bridesmaids. If any of the guests noticed that Rachel's eyes were pink-rimmed, they weren't tactless enough to ask why. James gave Bob to Mary as a wedding present. The newlyweds were often seen riding happily through the countryside until Mary found she was pregnant.

On February 28, 1845 Mary Angle Henry died giving birth to a dead child. She was buried in the cemetery behind the Evangelical United Brethren Church. His relatives had to restrain James from throwing himself into his wife's open grave, hacked from the frozen ground.

In the spring he had a slate gravestone placed on her grave. James visited the grave nearly every day, comforted by the thought that she was near him.

He was faithful to the memory of his Mary for what was a long time in those days. It had taken him a while to make up his mind to marry her. Now he took his time about deciding on her successor.

But on December 7, 1848, Rachel Hodge married James K. Henry. She wore a simple black dress, to show that she sympathized with Henry's loss. After the ceremony, they stood in prayer beside Mary's grave. A chill blast of air full of stinging ice crystals chased them back to their buggy drawn by Bob, fretful and shivering.

James and Rachel didn't visit the grave for the next week. Somehow it didn't seem so important anymore and they had better things to do. But on the morning of the seventh day, they were awakened by a pounding on the door. It was the man who dug the graves and set the stones and he was in a sweat.

"I think you better come quick. It's Mrs.—it's Mary's stone."

Rachel and James stood in the freezing wind and stared at the stone. There were deep prints etched in it that hadn't been there seven days earlier.

"It's a horsehoe," Rachel said. James just stared. She had to drag him away from the grave.

That night a farmer who lived nearby heard a keening wail float out of the cemetery. Shivering, he dared to look out his frosted window at the graveyard. He stood transfixed as he saw a ball of fire floating silently in the snowy air. Then it spurted up like a Roman candle and all was dark.

The next morning James kissed Rachel and went out to the barn to do his chores and feed the horses. She watched him through the window, dark circles under her eyes.

She did her morning chores quickly, then sat down to read her Bible by the stove. In the heat she dozed off, then awoke with a start. She glanced at the clock. James should have been back. She waited a few uneasy minutes longer, then wrapped her shawl around her and hurried to the barn.

The kettle on the stove shrilled but nobody came. From the barn came Rachel's screams as she cradled the body of her dead husband, his blackened face stamped with the imprint of a horseshoe—the same jagged figure that had appeared on Mary's tombstone. In his stall, Bob stamped and tossed his head and snorted.

You can still see the ghostly horseshoes on the stone of Mary Angle Henry at Otterbein Cemetery on Route 22.[3]

EUGENE

Not all dead men who haunt us are ghosts. Take the strange case of Eugene....

June 6, 1929, the body of a man about 55 years of age was found on the 3C Highway near the Borum road. Dr. C.E. Kinzel, the Clinton County coroner was called and certified that the man had died of natural causes. The only identification on him was a piece of paper with the address "1118 Yale Ave., Cincinnati" written on it. This turned out to be a vacant lot. The person living closest to the address was named Eugene

Johnson, so the mortician and owners of Littleton's called the corpse "Eugene."

Olin Moon, the mortician, said that "the regular method of embalming was used in preparing the unknown Negro man for burial"—which was delayed while the authorities tried to locate his relatives. None ever came forward, although Mr. Moon recalled that one person who viewed the body appeared to recognize him yet did not say anything.

Eugene was a popular local celebrity. Nearly a million and a half persons came to see the body as it lay in state in its own little house in the side yard of the Littleton home. Charter buses detoured to pay a visit to Littleton's. On holidays and during the summer people waited in line to view "Eugene".

"Eugene" received a new suit almost every year. Eventually a a wire screen was built across the room to protect him from curiosity and souvenir seekers. Several times he was kidnaped, but was always quickly recovered. He was even taken as far as Ohio State University in Columbus.

After that incident the Littletons began to feel that Eugene should be properly laid to rest. After 30 years it was unlikely that any relative was going to claim him and the pranks were detracting from the dignity of the business. Mr. Littleton purchased a lot in the Sabina Cemetery and paid for a handsome new suit, casket, and marker.

The day they laid Eugene to rest was a brisk, windy October day. The tent and casket-lowering equipment, artificial grass, and row of chairs for the unknown family were all in place. The Littleton Funeral Home hearse pulled up and eight men carried the coffin to the grave.

It was a simple, dignified service and while it laid Eugene to rest, it has not yet laid to rest the mystery about who he was.[4]

MARY JANE'S GRAVE

When I appeared at the Autumn Under Glass festival near Mansfield, it seemed as if every other person asked me about "Mary Jane's Grave." The story went that Mary Jane, who died in the 1800s, was a witch. Teenagers whispered the usual scary stories: If you jump over the grave and spit on the stone, within three days you'll have a bad accident or die.

Everyone knew someone this had happened to. In 1985, I was told, a teen couple defaced the witch's gravestone, leaving only the words, "Not dead, but sleeping." That same night, the couple was killed in a nightmarish car wreck. I began nodding mechanically each time I heard the story.

Then a man approached my table. He was an imposing gentleman with a fierce handlebar mustache and a skeptical gleam in his eye.

"You know this Mary Jane's Grave business?" he demanded. "Well, the land where her grave is has been my family's property since 1863."

And he told me how Mary Jane had been a Shawnee herbalist. She lived in a root and bark hut and died in 1823. He talked about her as if he had seen her only yesterday.

"She was crippled with arthritis, couldn't hardly move," said my informant. "Kids liked to harass her, call her a witch, but people followed her wherever she stayed to get her herbal remedies."

"Her grave's not where everybody thinks it is," he said with a twinkle in his eye. "Sure, there's a shale slab marker in the graveyard. But she's buried about 150 feet away, on the top of the hill, because she said she wanted to see the sunrise."

Did he believe in the stories about the dire penalties for desecrating her grave? He shrugged.

"In 1952 a young girl visited and was laughing and mocking at the grave. Two days later she was killed in a traffic accident."

The herbs are still there, said the man with the mustache. "Her gardens covered acres." And he told me how Mary Jane stood only four feet, four inches, "but she was shorter because of her stoop. She looked like a woolen ball in her sheepskin coat."

I wonder how he knew?

MEMORIAL SPIRITS

Players and spectators on the course at Muirfield Village Golf Club grumbled as rain interrupted the 1993 Memorial Tournament for the fifth straight year. Six out of the past seven years had been a soggy mess. Was there something about the Tournament that brought bad weather to central Ohio? Or was it something about the land itself?

Winnie Palmer [Arnold Palmer's wife] asked Jack and Barbara Nicklaus, "Is this golf course built on an Indian burial ground? Because if it is, it's the spirits that are causing the bad weather. You need to appease the spirits by putting a shot of gin on the tombstone of the one of the Indian chiefs."

There is a small cemetery—Mt. Zion Cemetery—at the edge of the club grounds, near the driving range. There are about thirty gravestones and it does not appear to be an Indian burial ground. The date on the main monument is 1805.

While insisting that he did not participate, Jack Nicklaus conceded that he agreed to drive Barbara to the cemetery and he focused the headlights of the car at the spot while their son, Jack II, held the umbrella for his mother.

When a reporter visited the cemetery late Friday afternoon, there was a half-filled goblet of gin at the base of the main monument. "By this morning," Jack Nicklaus joked, "it was three parts water and one part gin."

Tournament administrator Jim Wisler reported that Barbara not only placed the gin in the cemetery Thursday night, but during the rain delay Barbara and Tournament General Chairman Pandel Savic drove a quarter-mile south to the burial site of an Indian chief named Leather Lips, executed by Tecumseh's brother, the Prophet, and placed a shot of gin there.

"I figured I'd better go to the head honcho," Barbara said later. "It stopped raining before we left the tomb."[5]

And in 1994 the Tournament enjoyed incredibly perfect, sunny weather.**

**Note: The quotes in this story are taken verbatim from the newspaper account. I am not responsible for any potentially offensive remarks or stereotypes.

A LANE TO THE LAND OF THE DEAD

The Paulding County author of this chilling tale wished to remain anonymous. I will call her Joanna*.

The evening of August 12, Joanna arrived at Russ' house and announced that they were going to the cemetery. When they first discovered a mutual interest in the supernatural, Russ had dropped intriguing hints about an eerie, abandoned cemetery established in 1849. Russ had always refused to take Joanna there, but this night he agreed to go—after dark.

Russ took his raccoon-hunting flashlight and they set off. There were no houses or lights, only dense woods and fields along the four-mile gravel road to the cemetery. Joanna grew more and more uneasy. Civilization seemed very far away.

At the end of the road, Russ stopped the car by a road block and turned off the lights. Even sitting side by side, Joanna couldn't see Russ in the pitch blackness.

Taking their flashlight, Russ and Joanna got out of the car and began the walk through a tunnel-like lane through the woods to the cemetery. Their footsteps sounded very loud on the gravel. With each step, Joanna's terror intensified. Joanna dug her fingers into Russ' arm and was about to suggest they go back when Russ stopped suddenly and said, "What's that up there?"

About 40 yards ahead lay the cemetery. Something pale moved at the entrance.

Joanna watched for a moment, afraid of what she thought she was seeing and desperately searching for a reasonable explanation. Through her terror she felt an unmistakably evil, terribly malevolent presence.

"What is it?" screamed Joanna

"I don't know," Russ said, studying the thing that moved in the flashlight beam.

"It must be a dog, or an animal or something," Joanna suggested desperately, but as they watched it, they knew it walked on two legs. Joanna begged Russ to leave, but he wouldn't. She raced back to the car and watched as Russ began to slowly walk back towards her, always keeping an intent eye on the figure.

Once back at Russ' house they discussed what they had seen: It had a human shape, was tan-colored and yet insubstantial as it glided along the ground. Russ had seen two identical figures back in the cemetery, each about waist-high, although one grew to a height of about five feet.

The figure Joanna saw had come at them down the lane, pacing Russ as he walked back to the car. During those minutes, he watched the thing in the beam of his flashlight constantly, keeping about 35 yards between him and the figure.

There is a barbed wire fence across the entrance to the cemetery. The thing would have had to go over the fence to come down the lane, but the couple never saw it climb or step. And they heard no other noise except the "night noises" from the woods and their own footsteps.

Can evil be so insubstantial? Can a few figures, seen in a dim light, really be that menacing? Neither Joanna nor Russ has gone back to the cemetery. Even Russ, who claims to be fearless, refuses to go back. Joanna tried for a daylight visit to the cemetery, but Russ talked her out of it. She has felt "drawn" there and perhaps that is why it is best she not visit again.[6]

SINISTER SIMMS

Athens has long been a center of spiritualism and occult activity. In the last century Jonathan Koons built a spirit cabin where the spirits of a race of men older than Adam regaled guests with music, messages, and miracles. Another spiritualist group built a tabernacle on Mt. Nebo, a hill so close to Heaven, you could feel the breeze from angels' wings...

Today, Athens has a reputation for strange doings back in its hills and hollows and ancient cemeteries. Ohio University students are told the story of how "unholy persons" are buried beneath Wilson Hall. It is actually built on the same subdivision as the former site of a graveyard maintained by the Athens State Hospital. The site is surrounded by at least fifty other cemeteries within a 10- to 15-mile radius. The story goes that a student either died a mysterious death at Wilson or a mass murder occurred on the top floor. After that, no one could ever spent a peaceful night in the room where the death(s) occurred. Finally the room was sealed up and, to this day, no one knows its exact location. Wilson supposedly rests in the center of a pentagram, symbol of mystic power, formed by five local cemeteries.

Simms Cemetery is one of these. Overgrown and unused, local legend says that a "lynching tree" in the cemetery still bears scars from the hanging rope. As a curious student and his friends approached the tree, a hulking figure suddenly stepped out from behind the trunk, blocking their path. The man, who wore dark clothing and brandished a sickle, urged the students to leave and never come back. Other witnesses have seen the same guardian who warns them away. The spirit of the forest? Or gatekeeper to places best left unvisited?[7]

THE BECKONING FAIR ONE

She was described as "the raven-haired fair lady." Whether she really was dark and beautiful or whether this was just the formula for a wicked beauty, we will never know. But the story goes that Mary's second husband murdered her sadly retarded daughter from an earlier marriage. When he was hung for the murder, Mary, left with nine other children to feed and clothe and house, vowed revenge for his death.

One by one the children grew feverish and dry-mouthed. One by one, they died. After the third child died, the community leaders gathered behind closed doors. Epidemics were not unknown, but no one else in the village was ill. They decided on Old Testament justice—beat the Devil out of the woman. This they did, and two more children died the same evening.

The elders met again. This time, "Thou shalt not suffer a witch to live," was their text. They pursued Mary to the edge of the village and stoned her to death. One of the remaining children dropped in the dust behind the coffin and died that night.

Once again the council was called. Obviously the powers of darkness were much more powerful than they had realized—reaching out to claim victims even from beyond the grave. Stronger measures were called for. The elders drew straws. Then the chosen one, with his aides, carrying chains, shovels, and an ax, went to the churchyard under cover of darkness. The grave was shallow and it required little digging before the stench of death came wafting up out of the hole.

Someone held up a lantern. The woman's waxen face, mottled with bruises from her stoning, seemed twisted in a leer. Her long dark hair seemed to fill the coffin. The man who had pulled the short straw raised his ax and brought it down with a sickening crunch through her neck. For a moment the body seemed to writhe. Fresh blood gushed from the stump, soaking into the corpse's black dress, as one of them reached into the coffin and pulled up the head by its hair. He said later that it felt like a snake coiling around his wrist. Other men, wrapped the body round and round with chains, locking them on the corpse's chest with a padlock as big as a human heart.

"She'll not stir 'till Judgment Day," remarked the man with the ax. The others nodded as they dug a hole on the other side of the graveyard fence, a smaller hole, just the size of a baby's grave—or a head. In silence they filled in the graves and departed for their homes. If their wives noticed the evil-smelling dirt on their boots or the red spatters on their shirts, they said nothing. To talk about the dead woman was to give her power—power that had been cut off, when her head was severed from her body and buried in a separate grave.

The surviving children were sent to a relative somewhere in Pennsylvania. And Mary is said to walk the Coshocton County graveyard on nights when there is a full moon, chains jingling, crying piteously, searching for her head and her children.

Coon hunters swear they have seen her headless ghost and heard her shrill screams. One couple parked by the cemetery hoping for a glimpse of the ghost. They both saw something stirring down the lane from the car. A ghastly pale face? or a white-tailed deer? The husband went to investigate, but when he returned, it was his wife who was pale and hysterical.

"The ghost came to the car!" she gasped, "and beckoned to me to follow her!"

The woman had asked, "What in the name of the Lord do you want?" And the ghost told her what it wanted—something so terrible that the woman was never able to repeat the message.[8]

HIGH SPIRITS
Ghosts who just want to have fun

Late in the night on holidays and family birthdays, the local people say, the two old ladies stand by the head of the stairs and listen to their long-dead relatives holding their parties on the first floor. The silver clatters, the glasses tinkle, and the laughter comes up through the stairwell. No one in that house fears death, for to die means merely that one joins the family at their party in the dining room.
-Louis Jones-

Why shouldn't ghosts just want to have fun? These ghosts are the life—and soul—of the party.

A BALL AT COLUMBIAN HOUSE

Through the cold driving rain I could see the words "COLUMBIAN HOUSE" painted in two-foot-high letters on the wide of the tall, yellow clapboard building. I clicked open one of the three doors with a tiny hand-forged metal latch. The front parlor with its shiny green woodwork was warm and welcoming except for the gentleman in the portrait over the mantelpiece who sneered down at me over his high collar.

A pair of of chalkware roosters sparred on top of a secretary, ladies in frilled caps gestured from reverse glass paintings. A bent-wood antique high-chair and a tiny hair-covered trunk set the scene firmly in the 1820s when Columbian House was built by John Pray, founder of Waterville.

The dining room on the right was painted a cheerful watermelon pink. I admired the long oval tables set with snowy napkins and glass candle shades, the opalescent glass curtain tiebacks. It was a comfortable place to be with the rain and sleet pattering against the glass.

Peggy Parker who owns the inn with her husband Tom, came out to welcome me and tell me what she could. I immediately noticed a cold spot in the hall by the stairs.

"That might just be a draft," Peggy said, "but I've heard a child crying in the hall," she added. The bottom-floor windows are fitted with storm windows; outside a flag stood straight out from the pole, but I felt no drafts. Passing a dark little closet, an employee restroom, I shuddered.

There was another cold spot at the top of the stairs. I felt the windows; there wasn't enough air to account for the cold, although there was a slight draft coming from under the attic door. Peggy had showed me pictures taken at the top of the stairs, by the men's restroom, and by the attic door, which showed mysterious hazy figures as if someone were trying to materialize.

The three second-floor rooms displayed more antiques: a rope bed, a Texas Star quilt, even a casket with a plaster skeleton grinning out at me. Peggy unlocked the attic door and went off to seat a large group of guests. I climbed the attic steps, their edges worn by many decades of feet.

Upstairs it was the nineteenth century. I stood in a long, barrel-vaulted ballroom with lath showing through the pinkish stucco. Row upon row of chairs were stored there: here a balloon-frame with bulbous legs like a dowager in a hoopskirt; there, a cluster of spinster-plain cane bottoms. A pair of twin yellow pine fan backs seemed to nod together, gossiping. Others sat righteously upright, like church elders.

Two finely proportioned white-painted fireplaces faced each other across the length of the room. It was full of antiques: a tall spinning wheel, a spidery black parasol, a metal-bound trunk big enough to hold a man's doubled-up body, and a disturbingly realistic headless mannequin seated in a rocking chair.

The sash windows, still filled with panes of bubbly, hand-blown glass, shuddered in the brisk wind. The tops of the windows slanted tipsily—nothing was quite plumb.

It was a commodious high-ceilinged room, the only place of its kind in the 19th-century Northwestern Ohio wilderness. And a party was going on. I could see the dancers, some of the women in frilled bonnets of the same era as the portraits downstairs, the solitary fiddler perched on a table in the far corner. The dance looked like a reel: a pair of dancers facing each other, galloped sideways between lines of other dancers holding hands. My foot started tapping. Although I normally have two left feet, looking at the flushed, smiling faces, I almost fancied they smiled and beckoned to me to join the dance. At the door I turned and curtsied to the company with a flourish.

Feeling rather silly, back downstairs, I wandered through the tavern area with its turkey-print curtains, vibrant red walls and fireplaces identical to the ones in the attic. As I faced the hall, I saw a fair, curly-haired child in a little white frock toddling towards me. Its arms were outstretched, and it was crying to be picked up. I swallowed hard and looked away. I cannot stand to see a child cry—especially a long-dead child, far beyond my reach and comfort.

Most of the guests had gone, so I went into the kitchen to talk to Peggy, who with her husband Tom, bought the inn in September 1993.

Said Peggy, "I've experienced a smoky smell in the employees' restroom—not cigarette smoke, but..."

"...a smoldering smell," chimed in the cook.

"And a musty old smell," finished Peggy. "Doors some-times close behind you. You'll see people walking by, just out of the corner of your eye. I've heard a child crying in the hall. I've seen silverware fly off a table and scoot across the floor. Things go missing and then show up in unusual places, like the time I couldn't find my van keys which I had left on my desk.

'OK, keep em!' I told whatever-it-is and I took the other car. The next time I got in the van, the keys were lying in the middle of the driver's seat."

Peggy also told me about Delphine, a waitress at the Inn for over 20 years who followed a smoky figure she thought was a guest down the hall into the tavern area. Suddenly she felt death around the figure and she stopped at the doorway to the tavern. The figure dissolved.

Once, when a psychic came to visit, Delphine felt a sharp, piercing feeling in her stomach down in the basement. The psychic said that someone had been stabbed to death and buried there. Another time, as she was serving dinner in the main dining room, she heard the front doorbell and saw a couple in antique clothes standing in the front parlor. Since there are many historic re-enactment groups in the area, it isn't particularly unusual to have costumed visitors. She served a dish, then went to seat the couple. They were gone. She looked in the other rooms, but they had vanished. And if they went out the door, she didn't hear the bell.

The Inn has seen its share of deaths: The Sheriff used to bring prisoners down river to the county jail at Maumee. What is now the Ladies' Room was sometimes used as holding cell. Once a boisterous local drunk banged on the door, shouting that he was sick. The banging finally stopped and in the morning he was found dead. Ever since, the door to that room won't stay closed, says the story, although it bolted easily enough for me. Others say they have heard the ghostly drum of fists on the door.

A few years after the Inn was opened, a guest vanished from his room, leaving behind all his things. As the years passed, the room got a strange reputation for being haunted. Thirty years later a farmer on his deathbed confessed to the murder and told where he'd buried the body. The ghost of the guest is said to still walk the halls of the Columbian House.

The late Charles Capron, a past owner of the Inn, didn't know about the ghost until "I was awakened from a sound sleep by the noise of heavy footsteps coming down the hall. It was as if a man with heavy boots was walking there. I arose, lighted a lamp and looked out. At the same moment my caretaker did the same thing. We stood at opposite ends of the hall, facing each other, and the sound of footsteps continued to approach, as if a man were walking between us, but nothing could be seen."

One story says that a child died here in a cholera epidemic; it is this child, searching for its mother, who cries in the hall. I saw the child again, just before I left, as I stood in the front parlor. It was stumping down the stairs, clinging with one tiny hand to the railing, still crying. I flinched and turned away. There was nothing I could do.[1]

TIME IMPRISONED IN AMBER

If you hear plates dropping in the kitchen at Elinor's Amber Rose Restaurant, there's no guarantee that they fell from human hands.

Maybe they were playfully flung by the ghost. Elinor Sluzas, owner of Dayton's popular Eastern European restaurant at 1400 Valley St. says poltergeist problems are popping up.

"When some of my young workers leave at night, they have run back in with a wild story," Sluzas said, "They tell me that when they go to get into their cars in the back parking lot, they look up and see a young girl standing in the attic window. She has long black hair and is dressed in a white gown."

The building in which the restaurant has been operating since 1990 is 90 years old. Formerly it was owned by Sigmund Ksiezopolski, who raised six daughters and one son in family quarters upstairs.

Sluzas said that after the sightings of the "friendly ghost" were made, other interesting things happened in the restaurant.

"Plates would come crashing mysteriously to the floor. Once the music came on when no one was around. Another time, a light went out for no reason. And one lady who was upstairs told me she heard laughter and sweet singing in the area of the attic.

"Now I don't really believe in this hocus-pocus. But when they told me some of these things, I dropped my teeth," she said, "There were independent incidents experienced by different people, so I'm bound to think something is going on."

My husband and I were enjoying our plates of spicy sausage and potato cakes in the old-fashioned atmosphere at Elinor's Amber Rose when our seven-year old daughter came back from the restroom.

"Mom, is this place haunted?"

"Why do you ask?" I asked, a bit startled.

"Because I heard music—polka music—and people laughing and singing."

I noticed that the musak wasn't polka music.

"It must have come from the kitchen," said my husband.

"No, it was outside the window by the bathroom," the little girl insisted, "I looked out and heard people singing but there wasn't anyone there."

Intrigued, I went back to the bathroom. The only music I heard was the classical musak. And I couldn't hear any kitchen noises at all.

While shopping at a supermarket, Sluzas ran into Rose Losko, a daughter of Sig Ksiezopolski.

"I told her about the girl in the window, and she said, 'Oh, that's Chickee,'" Sluzas said, "Chickee was a nickname for the youngest daughter in her family, and she said that Chickee was active in the store, loved it, and spent her life living above the store, as she never married."

Sluzas said reports of Chickee's ghost are more fun than bothersome.

"Nothing vicious or scary is going on," she said, "This is just like a warm, snuggly feeling. This is more like the presence of an angel than a ghost. I think that those we love, and loving people, are always with us, spiritually."[2]

THE NEVERENDING PARTY

John Campbell came to the Dayton Country Club as Manager in 1980, living in the upstairs apartment in the Clubhouse.

Early one morning about 2 a.m. Campbell was awakened by the sound of voices and music.

"It wasn't a threatening sound, but rather that of a pleasant party: chit-chat, clinking glasses and a music that definitely wasn't from the 1980s. It sounded almost as if it were coming from the living room next door." Campbell made his way down the hall. The living room was dark and quiet. "Maybe the dishwashers are still working with the radio on," Campbell thought, but he found the kitchens locked up. Next Campbell went to the lobby where he asked the night watchman a few carefully worded questions. No, said the watchman, his radio wasn't on. And the dishwashers had left before midnight...

Back upstairs, Campbell looked out his front window at the surrounding houses. No lights were on; no sounds drifted across the lawn. Perhaps he had dreamed or imagined the whole thing. Whether dream or imagination, it happened a dozen more times in the next six years—and not just to Campbell. In 1983 Phil Fozo, the new Assistant Manager, shared the apartment for a few months. One evening Fozo cleared his throat and said,

"Don't look at me like I'm crazy when I ask you this; but do you ever hear voices up here at night? Not scary, but like people at a party? And when you go to look, there's no one there?"

And Fozo told Campbell of two instances when he and his girlfriend heard the party.

In the fall of 1985, shortly before leaving DCC, Campbell spent a last night in the apartment with his fiancee. About 2 a.m. she shook him awake, "What's that noise? Do you hear it? It sounds like a party!"

Campbell told her, "It's a special party—a party that's gone on ever since I came here. And there are guests who are having such a good time, they just can't bear to go home."

Does the Dayton Country Club host a never-ending party? When the lights go out and the buildings are still and empty, do the Life Members pull up the darkened drive in their phantom Stuz-Bearcats and LaSalles? Do they hurry up the steps, ghostly jewels glittering and shirt studs flashing, to sip one last cocktail, dance one last spirited fox trot?

TIME RUNS OUT AT THE CLOCK

The facade of Columbus' Clock Restaurant is astonishing: a Byzantine fantasy of stained glass and chunks of colored glass that spell out "Mott Brothers—Buffet and Billiards." It is a minor miracle that the elaborate stained glass has survived the years without alteration, but The Clock, the ultimate 1890s saloon, has a survival of another sort in its ghost.

It was a dark and stormy night in February, 1909. Col. Randolph A. Pritchard, noted man-about-town, card shark, and professional womanizer, sat alone at the bar. Gentlemen shunned him. Ladies, particularly those of the evening, were often kinder. A message came for the Colonel: someone to see him outside. Pritchard smoothed his mustaches and downed the last of his whiskey. He had known she would come. He stepped outside where a woman raised her arms in an embrace. Moments later the Colonel staggered back into the saloon and collapsed, his blood pooling on the mosaic floor.

A wronged woman with a keen sense of justice and a keener knife had stabbed Pritchard through the heart. Few people got a good look at her in the snowstorm raging outside. She fled in a carriage up High Street before anyone realized what had happened. All she left behind were the prints of her bare feet in the snow and a dead scoundrel.

Few mourned Col. Pritchard's demise. In the words of the paper of the time, he was "a torrid womanizer, a noted cheat at cards, and a scalawag in business." The fair murderess was never captured. Legend says she is condemned to return to The Clock each February and re-enact her escape, leaving her bare footprints in the new-fallen snow on the sidewalk.

And outside, the stopped clock marks the time—10:05—for eternity.[3]

THE GUEST

The elderly gentleman was dressed in a neat, if old-fashioned, white summer suit, and he paused in the living room doorway of the ornate house on Asbury Road in southwestern Clermont County.

Edward Marsh*, sitting in the parlor, glanced up, but assumed that the older man, who leaned on a cane, was an early arrival for their housewarming party being held that afternoon. Edward didn't recognize the guest. He supposed the man had been invited by his wife Lisa*.

Before Edward could welcome him, the visitor walked down the hallway to the kitchen where Lisa was preparing for the party. After a bit, Edward wondered why Lisa hadn't brought the distinguished gentleman back to the living room parlor for introductions and libations. He found his wife alone in the kitchen.

"What happened to the older man?" Edward asked, puzzled.

"What older man?" Lisa replied, her mind on her work.

Edward searched the house, but there was no one there.

The couple later learned that during big parties at the house, an uninvited but well-dressed guest would sometimes appear. The neighbors told them that he was a former owner, who had built the house using profits from his Philippine silver mines. The man, a lawyer and a judge, had paneled the walls of the home he loved with Philippine mahogany and he enjoyed dropping by for big parties.

HIGH SPIRITS

When I think of Maumee, I think of the trees arching in endless green tunnels that follow the curves of the river. The houses of Maumee have the upright, shuttered look of New England houses.

The Chadwick Inn is one of those upright buildings. It was built in 1837 by Levi Beebe as the "Commercial Building," a kind of old-time mall, for it was a drygoods store, public room, post office, general store and stagecoach stop on the Ft. Wayne/Detroit run. There was a ballroom on the third floor.

Now the restaurant revels in brass chandeliers, period fruit print wallpapers, and lace-draped sideboards. The decor is old-fashioned; the menu, up-to-the-minute sophisticated. The cream and blue dining room is reflected in French doors leading to the private party rooms. Yet there is a feeling of someone looking out of the darkness at the guests.

Many colorful stories have been told about the building. It was a bordello in the 1930s. When the floorboards were torn up during remodeling, workmen found thousands of bobby pins. The building was torched by arsonists in 1975. There was an "oral tradition" that the building's owner shot his wife and her lover when he caught them in bed.

I visited the Chadwick Inn one rainy afternoon. Owner Jim Hodulik took Linda and I on a tour, starting from the bottom up. The basement walls were uneven stone masonry with ceilings so low that even I had to stoop. Yet I was not frightened or uneasy. There was nothing in the basement.

Hodulik took us up the back stairs past rooms full of charred beams and insulation. Did I notice anything particular on the stairs? Hodulik asked. I didn't.

"One day," Hodulik said, "a busboy went to get something from storage. As he was going up the stairs, he met a young woman coming down.

"The busboy fled to the kitchen. 'I just saw a ghost swing from the rafters!' he gasped.

"The others jeered at him, 'Was she good-looking? Did you go swing with her?'

'No,' he gulped. 'she was swinging on a rope—by her neck!'

"At that he ran out of the building, and never came back."

We climbed higher and came out in the ballroom. Even though it was raining and overcast, the room was very light and airy, lit by tall windows. I vaguely sensed something in one corner of the room. Then I saw the bar—and the man standing beside it.

"There," I said to Hodulik, "There's somebody standing by the bar." The man wore a full-sleeved shirt with a high black stock collar. He also wore a square-bottomed vest, long pants, tiny steel-rimmed spectacles, and an unusual hat—sort of a squashed top hat, made of some light-colored material like straw or bleached beaver felt. There was something wrong with his mouth, as if he'd lost some teeth, but he was smiling and raising a glass to us in a toast.

I described the man to Hodulik, who smiled skeptically.

"What's he drinking?" he asked.

"I don't know what he's drinking," I said, taken aback by the question, "Some amber-colored fluid. Why?"

"The reason I ask is, back in May of 1986, I was in the ballroom on a Friday, setting up for a wedding reception on Saturday. I was the last to leave and the first in on Saturday. In the morning I found the ballroom chairs knocked over or tilted up against the tables. And I found a bottle of Jack Daniels and two glasses sitting on a table." He grinned. "We call the ghost Levi, after Levi Beebe who died in 1838."

Later, checking my costume references for the type of hat and vest the ghost wore, I came up with a date in the mid-1850s. Perhaps he was Jonathon Neely who established the Neely House in 1841, a tavern noted for excellent meals and hospitable service, still keeping a proprietary eye on his investment.

Apparently the poet was wrong who wrote, "Best while you have it use your breath/There is no drinking after death." For whether the ghost is Levi Beebe or Jonathon Neely, it seems as though the spirit has been nipping at the spirits at the Chadwick Inn.

THE THRILL OF FEAR
Ghosts who reach out and terrify someone

*What if the dead "return?" What if they refuse to go back
when we are through with them? What if they try to
take us with them?"*
-Anonymous-

THE BANSHEE

The Irish call her the Banshee. She can be a grey-haired
old woman who washes the bloody shirts of the dead in a
stream. Or a young woman with blood-red hair floating behind
her like a pall. But the screams are always the same: the brain-
splitting shriek keening through the night before dying away to
a sob. Before morning, someone will die.

Goody* in Springboro has heard the Banshee.

"It was like somebody outside the window screaming at
the top of their lungs, howling as loud as any human being
could. It woke up me and my husband. We both sat up and
looked out the window. There was nothing there except that
terrible screaming. It sounded like somebody pressed right up
to the screen, somebody who wanted to talk and could only
scream. And yet I don't think it was human. I called it the
Banshee.

"I went to the window and time stood still. There was
nothing to see, but it was just as real as a person standing
outside of the window. My husband got the feeling of an older
woman, a toothless woman, a crone, hanging onto the very end

of life. And she was trying to talk—only it was coming out moaning or a fingernails-on-the-blackboard kind of sound. It made us physically ill to hear it. I knew it was trying to tell me something. It went on for a good twenty minutes—that creepy, unearthly sound. After it stopped I stayed awake the rest of the night."

Goody pondered the meaning of the Banshee's visit for a long time. It wasn't until a year later, in August of 1992, that Goody's daughter admitted that she had nearly bled to death in a Florida hospital—on the very night the Banshee wailed.

THE TERROR THAT COMES IN THE NIGHT

It started with a nightmare—or so Harry thought. One hot night in July 1950, he stayed up reading after the rest of the family had gone to bed. When he finally lay down beside his sleeping wife, he was struck by a chill so intense his teeth clattered together.

When the cold had become almost unbearable, Harry saw a glowing ball of light suspended in the doorway. It moved towards him. Then the light misted and swirled into the luminous form of Harry's first wife Alice.

Harry stared. She had died eighteen years before, after a short, bitterly unhappy marriage. Yet here she was, wearing a flowing white robe, her dark hair tumbling over her shoulders, smiling at him, as beautiful as she had been in life. Transfixed, Harry forgot the cold and smiled back at her.

Then Alice's body began to turn. Suddenly he found her hovering above his body, her hands gripping his shoulders, her face only inches from his own. She smiled again and her face began to change.

Harry saw a dead-white mask with two fiery red eyes blazing from it like hellfire. He opened his mouth to scream; she darted forward and fastened greedily on it like a moray eel.

He was totally helpless, pinned under the weight of her body, which seemed to grow heavier by the second. He couldn't breathe—she was sucking the air from his lungs. Just as he thought he couldn't stand it another second, he was

suddenly released. Praying, gasping, and choking he sat up.
And far away Harry heard mocking laughter.

That was just the beginning. Alice began to visit him
twice a week. Each time she felt stronger.

A few months later Harry visited his sister Virginia.
Tormented, he told Virginia about the dreams. His sister didn't
know what to think. She knew he was sincere, but she tried to
make light of the dream. Ghosts in flowing white robes that
sucked a man's breath just didn't happen in 1950. This was the
20th century, after all!

Practical Virginia talked her brother into getting a physical. To humor her, he went—and passed every test. But he
didn't tell the doctor about the dream, and it continued to
plague him. His weight plummeted. He could barely walk or
drive a car. Finally in October, Harry told the doctor his dream
and was immediately scheduled for psychiatric tests at a
hospital near Youngstown.

Harry went to bed early while his wife Mary and Virginia
sat up chatting. But Harry, nervous and fretful, wouldn't sleep.
Mary and Virginia took turns giving him water, aspirins, and
company until about 3:00 a.m. when he finally dropped off.
Exhausted, the women went to bed.

But as Virginia drifted into sleep she heard a strange
sound. She rushed down the hall to Harry's room and snapped
on the light. Harry lay rigid as a corpse on the bed. His face
was bright red; his eyes literally bulged from their sockets. His
mouth hung open slackly as if he was either dying or dead.

As Virginia ran towards the bed, she got the shock of her
life. The moment she entered the room, her entire body felt
like it was encased in ice. She couldn't move. Even the blood
in her veins felt like ice-water.

Somehow Virginia threw off the paralyzing cold and
fought her way to the bed where she pulled her brother to a
sitting position. In that second, something writhed and twisted
between them, a misty grey mass that spiraled towards the
ceiling.

Freed from the strangling pressure, Harry gulped for air. They both heard distant wild laughter.

"My God, my God, what is that?" Virginia whispered.

"I've been trying to convince you all this time..." Harry replied weakly, and he closed his eyes. Virginia sat up with the light on, alternately praying for and cursing the being that was torturing her brother.

In the morning Virginia begged him not to go to the hospital. He shook his head heavily. "There might be a chance they can actually help me. But I swear I'll never tell anyone else about this nightmare. If you stood beside me and swore to the truth of this, you realize they would lock us both up."

So Harry went and was tested. He was told that he was perfectly normal except for being a little nervous. Happily, he went home.

A few days later, on November 1, 1950, Virginia went to visit her brother, only to find that Harry had had a heart attack in the early morning hours. He died before the ambulance reached the hospital.

Twenty years later, Virginia still wondered: Was the spirit that killed Harry really the vengeful spirit of Alice? Or did some undead creature take on the form of Harry's dead wife?[1]

THE KISS

Rose was spending the night at the PNG/Buckley House in Wilmington. She woke suddenly at 2:30 a.m. feeling like there was someone in the room. Then he appeared: a big, muscular man, about six foot five.

"He walked to my side and looked at me, pointed to the door and said, 'Get out, get out now!'"

Rose just stared, wondering if she was just dreaming. Naturally she found it hard to sleep the rest of the night.

The second night she slept on the opposite side of the bed, and was again awakened by a presence.

"I opened my eyes to see a female spirit floating in mid-air on her side, like she was lying next to me. She moved closer, and I felt her lips touch mine—not once, but twice. I could actually feel the wetness on my lips. She then smiled, touched my arm and was gone.

"Was the man warning me of the woman? Did she leave him for a woman and he was jealous? I don't know, but I haven't been back since."

HOLY GHOSTBUSTER

For the Reverend Gerald S. Hunter, it all began when he was introduced to Don* and Bev* who were looking for someone with an open mind to check out their house. Hunter and his friend John, a registered nurse from Ashland, visited the 1820s house which overlooks a magnificent valley about three miles south of Wooster. Walking into the house, Hunter felt as if he had stepped back in time some 100 years.

"It was a two-story house with an old-fashioned stone basement. Perhaps it was just the darkness of that late morning, but the entire house gave John and me an eerie feeling, as if our every movement was being watched."

Don and Bev, an educated, upper-middle-class couple, ushered the men into the living room for iced tea and strange tales. "The more they spoke, the more visibly nervous John became, and the less protected I felt."

Bev first saw their ghost at a party. "Looking into the sitting room she saw a man—or what looked like a man standing inside the doorway within the shadows. He was about 35 years of age, well-built, with red hair and a closely cropped beard. He was dressed all in black, in clothing from the last century.

"He was staring at Bev and smiling. It wasn't a pleasant smile but more of a taunting grin. Bev thought he looked like a nasty guy—not at all the type she would have invited to her party if she had the choice. They stared at one another for a few moments, and then he simply vanished."

Emily*, Bev and Don's teenage daughter, was alone in the house on a sunny Saturday afternoon. As she was cleaning her upstairs bedroom, she sensed a presence behind her and turned. The red-bearded man in black stood in her doorway. His arms were folded and he stood there with a smirk on his face, his eyes following her. With considerable presence of mind, Emily walked towards the door. He stepped aside and let her go by. She then raced downstairs in terror and waited outside until her parents returned.

Most people feel uncomfortable in the upstairs bath. Towels sometimes fly past the heads of guests. Bev and Emily both told of being grabbed in the shower by an unseen, lecherous hand.

The house also possesses an icy cold spot at the base of the stairs where, legend says, a sickly baby was murdered by his father who couldn't stand his crying.

One evening Bev got home late from work and decided to bake some cookies. As she entered the kitchen, the light bulbs blew. She replaced them; they blew again. Trying to calm her nerves, Bev turned on the radio and began mixing the cookies. Suddenly the radio station changed—two complete turns. As she went back to the cookies, the station changed again, from light rock to a Christian station she never tunes in.

Bev had it. She switched off the radio, then went upstairs and drew a bath. She put a classical music tape in the bedroom stereo and got in the water. Five minutes later the music stopped abruptly and there was a thud in her bedroom. The tape lay in the middle of the bedroom floor.

John and Hunter listened to the couple's stories then Don and Bev left, giving them the run of the house. The two men set up their equipment: a 35-millimeter camera with infrared film, thermometers, circuit testers, and several tape recorders. Going to the stairs, they found themselves immersed in a cold spot. They set up three tape recorders—one on the middle of the stairs, one at the top and one past two of the bedrooms. They turned on the machines and began asking questions which could be answered by one rap for yes, two for no.

"Are you there?"

A loud bang exploded on the tape.

John and Hunter moved a little closer together.

They sat and meditated, listening to the house, open for whatever contact the spirit desired. Hunter felt two hard, quick breaths on the left side of his face. He instantly opened his eyes.

"I could see the family dog backing away from the stairway and into the living room below. The hair on his back was standing up, and he was growling and snarling as he seemed to watch some invisible being walk across the room."

That was enough. John and Hunter spent the next two hours in frenzied conversation, trying to distract themselves. Two days later Hunter contacted Alex Tanous, a psychic and investigator at the American Society for Psychical Research in New York. Tanous said he had an impression of an undesirable and unpleasant man named George who still considered the Wooster home his and resented anyone living there.

Then Hunter phoned a Michigan psychic who told him that the ghost's name was George and he had lived in the house around the 1890s. At this Hunter's hair stood on end. George's wife's name, she said, had been Martha or Marsha. He had been a cruel and abusive husband. The psychic also sensed the death of a child in the house and that George's wife had died of grief rather than live with such a terrible man. George still believed the house belonged to him and he wanted Bev and Don out.

After this Hunter went to the County Records office at Wooster. The old land deeds said that the house was owned in 1900 by a man named George and a woman named Martha.

"I felt as though I had just opened a crypt. In great excitement, I phoned Bev and told her I had discovered the name of her ghost."

"She told me I was too late. It seems the night before, her son was playing with a Ouija board, and had asked the name of the ghost in their home. The board spelled out 'George.'"[2]

SHE TOUCHED ME

Wanda Parr wrote:

One night as I lay beside my husband at my parents' home in Navarre I saw something white moving in the room next to ours. At first I thought it was a curtain, but as it got closer, I could see that it was a woman in a white wedding gown and veil, floating above the floor.

I had lived in this house for over ten years and my father had often told of seeing an apparition like this at the foot of his bed which he called a "Madonna." I hadn't paid much attention, but now I was suddenly filled with fear.

Although I was afraid my husband would say I was crazy, I shook him awake and asked him to get out of bed and turn on the light. The switch was by the doorway, just where I had seen the figure. Half-asleep he began to stumble towards the light switch. He never made it. Suddenly he screamed,

"She touched me! She touched me!"

I started screaming too and my father came racing up the stairs and switched on all the lights, convinced we were murdered each other! My dad finally got us both downstairs which was quite a job since my husband was shaking uncontrollably, repeating, "She touched me and it was ice-cold!"

I felt terrible. I had no idea he would see her too—and I had let him walk right into her! He was furious with me! We never slept upstairs again and even though we don't live there any more, we still do not sleep without a light on.

We later learned that a young girl had been murdered fifty years before with an ax in the backyard. The room we shared had been her room.

THE WEB OF FEAR

During Marge's* first week in the turreted Victorian house in Youngstown, she and her family were so exhausted they didn't notice the presence that lurked there. It wasn't until the second week that she noticed a damp, foul odor throughout the house. Scrubbing the walls top to bottom didn't help. She finally blamed the smell and the damp on the many trees overshadowing the house. But that didn't explain the soft moaning sounds, the muted sobbing that they heard even when there was no wind to stir the trees. Their nights were nightmarish with footsteps overhead in the empty attic and things going bump in the night.

By the following July the house had learned several new, unpleasant tricks. Whenever Marge went into the cellar, the air thickened and swirled around her like a veil, smothering her.

And on the attic stairs, between the first step and the ceiling, grew a thick grey cobweb. Once a week Marge would sweep it away, watching for the monster spider that could spin such a web. Yet, the next time she opened the attic door, the web would be back, thicker and more shroud-like than ever, moving obscenely, vaguely alive.

In August, Marge went down into the cellar to do laundry. Suddenly she was smothering in a thick invisible blanket. Blind and suffocating, she groped her way up the stairs and was able to breathe in the kitchen.

That same evening Marge's brother Frank arrived for a week's visit. He was a minister and when Marge and her husband poured out the strange events in the house, he gently suggested that they were suffering from overactive imaginations. Seen through his rational eyes, the couple realized, their ghostly mysteries could all be easily explained away.

Late that night, after everyone had gone to bed, Marge's was shocked awake by her brother's hoarse screams. She found him standing on the attic stairs clawing madly at his face which was completely enveloped in the giant grey cobweb.

When the web was cleaned away and Frank had stopped shaking, he explained that he had been awakened by a voice calling his name over and over. "I got out of bed and went into the hall. I must have mistaken the attic door for your bedroom door and when I opened the door and walked in, I got tangled in that shroud! Naturally I panicked. What a horrible dream! Your stories really must have preyed on my mind. I've never had a dream like that one and I've never sleepwalked in my life."

The next day and night were quiet. But on the third afternoon, the house struck again. One after another fires flared up spontaneously in the corner of the living room. The family was at their wits' end. Marge scarcely slept that night.

But Frank did sleep—and he dreamed. The next morning he told her that he had prayed for an answer to the house's sickness.

"In my dream I thought I was in the attic, wrapped in the cobwebby stuff I was entangled in the other night. In the corner of the attic was a blazing fire that grew and grew in size. I was trapped there."

Frank was convinced that the dream was a warning. He believed that the house was a place where the forces of Evil had entrenched themselves. "You and your family must not be here when the Light begins to cast out the Evil," he warned and Frank insisted the family pack and leave with him at once.

Marge got her first good night's sleep since they had bought the house. They put the house on the market, telling each prospective buyer of the strange events. The buyers looked at them as though they were mad, but the house sold quickly for it was 1944 and there was a housing shortage. The new family lived there exactly one month, then moved. After a long vacancy, the house was sold to a fraternal organization who completely remodeled it and opened it as a club.

Marge saw the fulfillment of Frank's prediction sixteen years later. On December 1960 the clubhouse was completely destroyed by a fire. The investigator ruled, "cause of fire unknown."

The fraternal organization built a new building on the same site. To this day it is untroubled. The forces of Good have apparently triumphed. But where did the Darkness go, when it was driven out by the Light?[3]

MANY MANSIONS

It was a steamy day in late summer, 1993. My friend
Linda, who describes herself as "psychically deaf," drove me
past the excessively Victorian building on Toledo's
Collingwood Boulevard. Its elaborately carved window frames
and mansard-roofed tower were straight out of an Addams
Family cartoon. The paint was slipping off the tower clapboard
and peeling off the brick, giving it a leprous, scabby look.
There were no lights in any of the windows.

Eric Beach and Jim Beard met Linda and I outside the
darkish-brick Romanesque building. Two blank stone shields
on the upper walls seemed awaiting funeral inscriptions.
Greenish with age, the high-pitched tile roof was as pointed as
a witch's hat. Something white in one of the tiny windows
high in the dormers gave the impression of a pale face peering
out.

As we walked through the doors, there came the familiar
blow in the face, and the sensation of something pressing down
on my back, forcing me to hunch my shoulders. Inside, a long
corridor lined with what had been nun's cells, led to the Arts
Center office. Eric and Jim kept up a running commentary on
the building's history.

The Ursulines, a teaching order of Roman Catholic nuns,
founded their first convent and school in Toledo on Cherry
Street in 1854. In 1905 the Ursulines moved the school to this
architectural nightmare. Mary Manse College, a small liberal
arts college, opened here in 1922. It closed its doors in 1975.
The building was used as a nuns' convalescent and retirement
community until 1985 when Pat Tansey, a local art-lover who
had dreams of saving the building, decided to create a community arts center. He rented the building from the Ursulines and
opened it as a place for artists to live and work. Now potters,
poets, and painters rent apartments and studios, give classes,
and hold shows in the labyrinth of rooms and corridors.

As we started up one set of steps, I got a nasty shock. On
the darkened landing was a statue of St. Angela Merici, the

founder of the Ursuline order, her waxen face unnervingly like that of a garishly painted corpse.

"What do you want to see first?" Eric asked.

Seeing anything was the last thing on my mind, but "Let's get the worst over with first," I said with bravado, "The basement."

Linda and I were led through a maze of corridors and backstage scenery flats, arriving at a small doorway leading to the basement stairs. Jim unlocked it and I found myself looking down into darkness. Jim flipped a switch, then apologized and went down into the dark to find a light. The bulb was burned out. "That happens too often on this particular stairway," he said.

It was on this staircase that Tina came face to face with the faceless—a dwarfish figure in a hooded black robe gliding directly up the stairs at her. She slammed the door just in time.

"Isn't there another way into the basement?" I muttered feebly. They gallantly led me to another stairway, past a sweeping stair to the theatre balconies where St. Michael trampled the devil in a niche. The hooded figure has also been seen on this stairway, on the first floor of the theatre, in the lobby, and coming out of the elevator.

Shrinking down the stairs into the low-ceilinged basement, I immediately began to have trouble breathing. Something seemed to be wrong with my eyes. Linda took hold of my wrist and led me.

"Just keep breathing," she said, "just keep breathing."

It was too dark in the basement. There were lights on, but I couldn't see them. The men pointed out strange symbols drawn on the cement. Years before, while the building stood vacant, undesirables had stolen into the basement and used it for occult ceremonies, apparently conjuring up something very old and not quite human.

"And over here," said Eric, pointing the way "is where the hooded figure always vanishes. Come and see..."

Involuntarily I took a step backwards. "Over my dead body...." I thought. It was becoming harder to think.

Linda said that at that point her hair stood up. All we wanted were flashlights to shine into corners and dispel that dark. Instead we walked into the laundry room, full of huge washers and driers like iron lungs. Stepping over the threshold, I was suddenly free of the pressure on my head. "It's all right in here," I said, breathing again.

Jim and Eric nodded wisely. "It always is."

They theorized that the traffic in the laundry room has kept its atmosphere clearer than the rest of the basement. As Eric was folding his laundry one night, he saw the hooded character—about five foot seven inches tall—apparently the dwarf had grown—with its gliding walk. At least seven other people have seen it, he added.

Next we visited the high-Victorian building I had seen as we first drove by. It's called Gerber House after Christian Gerber, a local merchant who spared no expense when he built it in 1872. Linda and I admired a huge Eastlake fireplace and mirror surround carved in burl walnut, a white marble rococo - revival fireplace in the back parlor, the walnut staircase to the third floor. Darkened metal hands protruded surreally from the wall, clutching air. "They used to hold gas-light torches," Eric explained.

A ghostly bride has been seen in this beautiful parlor. One spring evening, five tenants of the Arts Center were enjoying dinner at a table in the front room. From the back closet, a swirling white mist began to form. Speechless, the diners watched as it moved forward, becoming clearer with each movement. The specter, dressed in a wedding gown, was clearly visible before it vanished at the pocket doors.

Was she a bride of the Gerber family, a former student, being married in the school parlor? Or could she have been a young bride of Christ, symbolically dressed in wedding gown and veil for the sacred nuptials when a postulant becomes a novice? Did she die before she was able to take her final vows? We may never know; she has never spoken to anyone.

In the north rooms of Gerber House, small children have been seen running in and out of the back closets—formerly doors to rooms now part of the theatre. Residents consider the children harmless. They only ask that the doors be left open to the hall, so that they may roam freely through their former home. As she passed by the door to Gerber House, Jim's wife Becky felt someone walk through her. "She actually felt a human form," Jim said, "It tickled her and she laughed out loud."

Upstairs were rows of dismal little rooms, identical in their brownish walls and air of depression and loneliness. I tried to imagine living there when the building had been active and full of life. I couldn't. The air in these rooms was dead.

We walked a curving corridor lined with deep cupboards. I opened one at random, half-expecting to find something dead wrapped in old newspapers. The floors were scarred wood, like a skating rink. I had a sudden nightmare vision of nuns gliding silently towards us on rollerskates.

Somehow we emerged onto the balcony above the theatre, a large room topped with a stained-glass dome, its box seats now turned into tiny stages topped with miniature baroque canopies. The theatre was dark. But something darker sat in one of the rows. Head down, staring at in seat in front of her, was a nun.

"There's someone down there," I whispered to myself.

She turned an ash-white face towards us. I have never felt such malevolence in my life. I don't know what she wanted. All I know is that she hated and could do nothing but hate without even death to release her. "Lord have mercy on us all," I murmured.

Nearly a year later, I opened the synopsis of ghost stories Eric had given me when he first invited me to the Center. There he had written: "There is something dark in the back rows of the theater. Usually malevolent, it throws sparks and images at those who invade its space. Sometimes it can be felt in the balcony as well."

I believe this dark nun stalks the halls and cells of the old convent. Eric also wrote, "a tenant, who never wished to believe in the supernatural, was walking through the second floor of B-Wing on her way to the soda machines. As she approached the middle of the passage, she noticed a distortion—a 'molecular windstorm' in front of her. It came right at her! As it passed through her, a fierce anger rose in her; then a chilling cold as if she were in a crypt. She spent the rest of the night in bed, talking herself out of what just happened."

We took an elevator to the attic. Again, the lights in the hall refused to work. We turned to a vista of arched doors extending the length of the attic. These were the workrooms, skylights set into their slanted ceilings, making the rooms light and airy, despite the heaps of old clothes, scraps of heating duct, and trash. Each room was linked by an open door, the varnished woodwork echoing down to the end of the building.

As I admired how much the view looked like an artist's exercise in perspective, another nun leaned around the final doorframe. She was a good-humored-looking woman with the strangely ageless face nuns sometimes have. She had a pile of sewing on her lap; one hand was poised in mid-air as if holding a needle, with the other, she gave a little wave and she smiled.

In that smile was a love that transcended time, a human warmth I hadn't felt anywhere else in the building. She was not dead, but still following the Rule, busy at her sewing in the Motherhouse workroom.

Perhaps, I thought suddenly, this is Heaven: to spend an Eternity being about your Father's business.

We made our way back outside. It had grown dark. Thunder rumbled far off and a warm rain was beginning to fall. I had a splitting headache and suddenly all I wanted was to get away. The building had drained me. Traveling from Hell to Heaven in the space of a few hours was too much for one day.

As we drove off, I wondered who watched us from those dormers, now glazed black with storm clouds—the dark nun, trapped in a hell of hatred, the inhuman hooded creature, or the nun in the workroom, Love made visible.

"In my Father's house are many mansions..." Is there room for all?

THE FACELESS HITCHHIKER

The place is known as Dead Man's Curve. Built in 1831,
it was a narrow, curving, two-lane road called the Ohio
Turnpike and it had a long list of victims. In 1968 the authorities decided to tame its death-dealing curves. In September of
1969, the wide, four-lane road was officially opened; the
authorities congratulated themselves on eliminating Dead
Man's Curve. On October 19, 1969, five people died there.

Rick, his best friend Bill, and another teen, Danny, had
been to see a football game at Goshen. As they drove Bill's
two-door 1968 Impala down a country road, Rick suddenly felt
tired and uneasy. He told Bill he wanted to go home. Oblig-
ingly Bill turned the car around on a side road, then pulled up
to the stop sign on Dead Man's Curve. He looked both ways.
He pulled into the middle of the road. It was 1:20 a.m.

As he pulled out, the car was broadsided by an eastbound
1969 green Roadrunner with no lights. Police later estimated
the car's speed at 120 to 140 mph. Rick was the only survivor.

He has lived with this horror for the past twenty-five years.
And the horror continues to haunt him and his friends in a very
tangible way. For since that dreadful October night, the
creature they call "the faceless hitchhiker" has haunted Dead
Man's Curve.

It is a dead-black figure of a man a "three-dimensional
silhouette" as Rick describes it. He has seen it six times in
twenty-five years. The first time he had stopped to let a friend
use the bushes. His friend came flying back to the car, the
black Thing behind him.

In 1974 Rick was stopped at the same intersection where
the accident occurred. No cars were visible in either direction.
He suddenly saw the dark Thing spring out of a clump of
cattails in the ditch. He was so spooked that he pulled into the
road, where the car was shaken by the wind from a passing
car—a 1969 green Roadrunner.

Rick's friend Todd told me, "Rick and I were heading
home to Bethel from Amelia. I noticed a man's shape on the
side of the road. It turned like it was hitchhiking, with an arm

sticking up. The thing wore light-colored pants, a blue shirt, longer hair—and there was just a blank, flat surface where the face should have been. We looked back. There was nobody there. I've also seen the black shadow figure, walking its slow, labored, dragging walk by the side of the road."

Rick hired a clairvoyant from Pittsburg, who had never heard of the place. He dropped her off in broad daylight on a sunny afternoon. "Just leave me here for a couple of hours," she said. Rick drove home—a ten-minute drive. Five minutes later, the clairvoyant called him from the deli up the road. "Just get me the hell out of here," she said. She told Rick that it was the worst place she had ever encountered. "Someone very evil is there. He died suddenly and he is still there."

Sherry*, a friend of Rick's, was driving her mother's station wagon along the road at 1:20 a.m. The black Thing ran out of the woods and threw itself in front of her car, trying to block it. She hit it and felt both sets of wheels lift, like "running over speed bumps twice."

"My God, I'm a nurse. I could have killed somebody!" she said to herself and started backing up. As she looked in her rear-view mirror, she saw the Thing putting a foot on the trunk, grabbing the luggage rack to climb up on the top of the car. She floored it. Even now she gets the shakes when she talks of that night.

The faceless hitchhiker's spell extends even beyond Dead Man's Curve. One night as Rick, Todd, Andy, and Paul were heading east on 275 between the Montgomery and Loveland exits, "a two-door 1968 Impala came right up on our tail with its high-beams on. He backed off a little, then did it again. I thought he was going to ram us. Then the car passed and swerved towards us. I'm over six foot and I got a good look into the driver's seat. There was nobody driving that car," said Todd.

The hills and hollows of Clermont County hold many secrets. Some keep their secrets unto death. But the final chapter in the story of the faceless hitchhiker will never be told until the Judgment Day.

APPENDIX 1
FRIGHT BITES
Mini-tales of the macabre

I had so many stories I decided to tantalize you with skeletal snippets from around the state. You may want to investigate some of these on your own. By the way, when I say "the ghost haunts" I mean, "the ghost is *said* to haunt."

Every midnight in Falls Twp., Hocking Co., you can hear the scream of a man killed decades ago in a drilling accident.

An elderly woman materializes and pulls silverware drawers out in the Trilby house where she and her sister were brutally beaten to death during a robbery.[1]

A Williams Co. cemetery is haunted by a landlocked sailor who whistles "Blow the Man Down."[2]

A headless horseman haunts Cherry Hill or Ghost Hill in Fayette County. His head was cut off by robbers, who found his body missing when they pretending to "discover" his death.[3]

An Indian girl who was accidentally killed by one of the men fighting for her hand, haunts a swamp near New Carlisle, in the form of a ball of blue light. Smithsonian excavators dug up a skeleton with a crushed skull, but the ghost still walks.

Near the Lake Vesuvius blast furnace, workers were startled to find the Devil in human form blocking their path. The furnace owners brought in a priest to deal with It. He asked the Devil, "What in God's name do you want?" No one has ever recorded the Devil's answer.[4]

Near Yellow Springs a headless Civil War soldier, Charlie Batdorf, has been seen walking down the path to his house.[5]

Shunk, near the Maumee River, is haunted by a gigantic Indian warrior on a ghostly white stallion, who was killed so he could guard $40,000 in gold buried on the banks of South Turkeyfoot Creek. Treasure hunters have reported being trampled by his horse.[6]

On W. Water St. in Greenville, an Indian girl who committed suicide after she was assaulted by soldiers from Ft. Greenville, haunts the large boulder where she was buried.[7]

Dead Dog Island in Port Clinton was a swampy area where local authorities used to dump dead animals and trash. When a family built a house on the other side of the marsh, an old man warned them that they were disturbing the spirits of the dead animals and would be harmed if they didn't move. After several accidents, the house caught fire and burned to the ground; a pack of wild dogs kept firefighters from reaching the house.

A ghostly soldier called "Gory Head and Bloody Bones," mutilated at St. Clair's Defeat haunts the Peace Rock area of Ft. St. Clair.[8]

A ghostly soldier and his wife have been seen strolling hand in hand or sitting under a huge oak tree on the Eaton-Gettysburg Rd. The young wife had a stake driven through her body by the Indians and died near the tree.[9]

Galion's old train depot, particularly a sinister little room on the second floor known as "the coffin room," is haunted by a ghostly man in a long coat and an "inhuman thing." Ghostly trains have been heard and felt shaking the building.[10]

At Miamiville the ghost of a trainman killed by Morgan's Raiders has been seen on the tracks, in the road, and watching a farmer plow his field, as if lonely for life.[11]

The Abbott Mausoleum in the Milan cemetery supposedly holds a rocking chair, photos, and other personal possesions of Mr. and Mrs. Abbott. If you disturb the Abbots by knocking on the door, they will chase you.[1]

Sylvania's Ravine Park Cemetery is haunted by a bride who can't rest because her family couldn't decide which of her three husbands to bury her by.[13]

A ghostly lake-boat captain stumps around Joy Cemetery in Ottawa Hills looking for his missing wooden leg.[14]

The Alpha Xi Delta sorority of Marietta College is haunted by a ghost named "George" who appears as a man in an old-fashioned brown suit on the second floor. He is believed to be George White, an Ohio governor in the late 1930s.[15]

Old Man Rowe, the hermit of Old Man's Cave, is said to haunt the cave to guard the treasure he buried there.[16]

A ghostly equestrienne rides the "Military Horse" on the Frontier Carousel at Cedar Point Amusement Park. She is believed to be either Mrs. Daniel Muller, wife of the carver or a woman who fell in love with the horse on her honeymoon. The horse cannot be photographed without some mishap.[17]

The Village House Restaurant in Ashville appears to be haunted by the late owner who pulls pranks like squirting hot water from the coffee urn.[18]

Carroll County's once-magnificent Cox Mansion was said to have been built by Isaac Cox to impress his wife's father. The day it was completed, Cox said, "Here's your house, dear," and either dropped dead or committed suicide. A young woman is said to drift down the 60-foot tower's staircase playing the violin. A headless horseman has been seen riding through the orchard, and organ music and a crying baby have been heard in the tower.[19]

Nicodemus was a runaway slave who was killed when he was discovered in a secret tunnel in what is now the Zeta Tau Alpha sorority, 24 E. State St. One woman was awakened by a large, muscular arm trying to strangle her. Another felt someone in bed with her. But when the women began leaving soothing notes to Nicodemus, he settled down.[20]

At the horse pasture behind the Blue Jacket Ampitheatre outside Xenia, an actor playing his Indian drum felt Indian spirits come out of the woods to listen. When he stopped, they retreated. During performances, watch for actors that mysteriously disappear.

Dayton's Ridge Street Bridge is haunted by Bessie Little, shot by her lover and thrown into the river. You can hear her falling over and over to her death.

A phantom house has been seen at Sugarcreek Reserve in the early 1990s with lamplight shining through its windows. Another was seen in the 1950s on the side-lawn of the United Methodist Church in Crown City, Lawrence County. When approached, these houses simply melted away.[21]

A teacher named Rachel lived in a tiny 1804 stone cottage in Centerville. Once known as the Buck's Horn Tavern, it had sheltered William Henry Harrison in 1812 and slaves traveling the Underground Railroad. Rachel saw a woman in a light blue ruffled dustcap, a long, full-skirted light blue dress, and a white apron. She smiled at Rachel, said, "I live here, too, you know." and vanished.[22]

The Old Courthouse of Dayton still houses the gallows used for the last public execution in Montgomery County. Volunteers have reported the sound of footsteps trudging slowly up the steps to the Judge's Chambers, then a soft moaning.

The Old Stone Front Home in Piqua was haunted by a child who sobs bitterly. He was abducted, along with a large sum of money, on the evening before his mother's funeral. Twenty years later workmen digging out a well found the delicate bones of a child.[23]

Beaver Creek State Park is haunted by "The Mushroom Lady" who poisoned the man she loved and his fiancee with deadly mushrooms in a stew. Human bones have been unearthed and strange images have turned up on photographs. Nanette Young and a friend rode to the site and found no trace of their previous day's visit where there should have been footprints and hoofmarks.

On Lima's South Sugar St., Maryanne and her two cousins saw a transparent elderly lady with gray hair piled on top of her head, wearing glasses and earrings. She had a wine glass in her hand and was talking with about six other people in the kitchen who also had cocktails in their hands.[24]

Ft. Hayes in Columbus is haunted by a young private blown to bits by an overheated cannon fired for Lincoln's 1865 lying-in-state. The soldier was in love with the daughter of his commander, who supposedly knew the cannon would explode. A ghost in WWII uniform also haunts the Fort.[25]

Mother Angela Sansbury—Mother Sans—haunts Sansbury Hall at Ohio Dominican in Columbus. Fearing fire, she walks the halls and switches off hairdriers, curling irons and other appliances. She also waters students' plants.[26]

On Ludlow Avenue in Cincinnati stands a pseudo-Tudor house once used as a gangsters' "pleasure palace." In the 1920s, rival mobsters gunned down two women and stuffed their bodies into a third-floor closet. On the anniversary of the women's death the odor of rotting flesh can be smelled on the third floor.[27]

A fire chief named Laudenbach haunts Engine Three firehouse. A firefighter new to the house saw him putting on a pair of waterproof pants by his old locker. He followed him down the stairs, heard the pants swishing, then the man disappeared. Other firefighters confirmed that Laudenbach had died on that same date 15 years earlier.

The ghost of Mary Emery haunts the Emery Mansion. Emery, who built the community of Mariemont, worked to eliminate class distinctions and religious bigotry. Somehow this got twisted into a story that Mary Emery hated Catholics although the Emery mansion passed from a family trust to the Sisters of Charity. A nun, working late, came face-to-face with the ghost of Mary Emery, who glided down the huge staircase, pointed a finger at the nun and whispered, "Get out."[28]

Blood House, in Clifton, is haunted by smoky, vaguely human figures in the bedrooms, little girls in the hall (the building was once a girl's school), and footprints in fresh snow that simply stop, traces of a murderer who killed his wife, then left bloody foot-prints in the snow.[29]

Evna of Akron told me of dirty doings at her mother's Stark County house. "Mom and Dad built the house fifty years ago. After Dad died, Mom watched a lot of TV. The ghost would change the channel to a football game or a religious station, especially during *Rosanne*! One time, my Mother's new boyfriend had just gone home. When she came back from the kitchen, she found white footprints on the dining room rug, tracking from the front door to the telephone and back. She touched the prints; they were grainy, like sand. She thought it was strange that she hadn't noticed him tracking dirt in before. She went into another room to get the vacuum cleaner. When she came back the tracks were gone."

A man with shoulder-length white hair and a full white beard wearing a black suit, wire-rimmed spectacles and a wide-brimmed Quaker hat has been seen in the dining room of the Hass Home in Waynesville.[30]

In the elegant Italianate Douglas Putnam house in Marietta now known as "The Anchorage," Eliza Putnam, a shadowy figure dressed in a long gown, lingers on the stairs near the dining room.[31]

A ghost in a blue uniform haunts the auditorium at Circleville's Memorial Hall. He has been seen in mirrors and frequently flushes the toilets in the rest rooms. Circleville historian W.W. Higgins wonders if he is a Civil War Veteran, one of the G.A.R. who built Memorial Hall in 1890.

The Mansfield house Nadine grew up in was built in the 1920s. Wrote Nadine, "Routinely, my sister and I would hear footsteps in the attic or scratching on the inside of the attic door. We would call Dad upstairs and he would go up to check but, of course, no one was there. Since the attic door was next to the bathroom door, this made us very nervous. When I was about four years old I went upstairs to the bathroom by myself. I wasn't tall enough to reach the light switch in the bathroom, but my Mom always left a light on in their bedroom which shone across the hall. As I sat there, a shadow ran across the bathroom floor. But it wasn't the shadow of a human—in fact the best description would be that of a six-foot tall praying mantis."

A Miami Indian chief was said to haunt St. Clair's Creek (now Sevenmile Creek) and paddled his birch canoe at high water times. His painted face was so terrifying that people who saw him fainted.[32]

Below the Fort St. Clair graveyard in the ravine is a haunted spot where an Indian can be seen dancing around his fire in the full moonlight.[33]

The great werewolf flap started July, 1972, in Marion County with what must have been the original stinky cheese man: a 7-foot monster which smelled like limburger cheese. A woman motorist reported to the sheriff's department at Upper Sandusky that a big, black thing jumped out of a ditch right beside her car. In the last week of July, 1972 three witnesses told police they saw a 9-foot beast lurking along the railroad tracks near downtown Defiance. A train crewman said that he was hit from behind with a two-by-four, injuring his shoulder. When he ran, the "werewolf" fled into some bushes.[34]

Library Park in Miamisburg was, and may still be, haunted by a ghostly murder victim in a white dress. In 1894 the apparition was seen almost nightly by thousands of people, floating through the tombstones of the Miamisburg Cemetery—a young woman in white hands clasped behind her, head bent in deep thought. She has been seen as late as the 1980s.[35]

Nobody can really tell me why Carpenter Road in Greene Co.

is so spooky. The most common version tells of a ghostly farmer
driving a ghost tractor.

US 27, in the western part of Butler County, has been called
"the Highway to Heaven" because of numerous fatal accidents on
the road. A ghost motorcyclist has been reported, coming head on
at motorists. At the last moment the motorcycle soars over the top
of the car and disappears.

On Princeton Road (Ohio 129) near Hamilton, motorists have
reported the ghost of a woman standing or walking beside the
road. She warns drivers of danger near the spot where she was
killed in a traffic accident. If the driver slows down or stops, the
ghost will hitch a ride.

The Screaming Bridge is at Princeton Rd. and Maud-Hughes
Rd, east of Hamilton in Liberty Township. Some say the noises
are produced by rain grooves in the bridge. Others say the screams
are those of people who have died on or near the bridge. Ghostly
figures and glowing red balls of light as well as lights on a
phantom caboose have been seen.[36]

At Spook Hollow near Oregonia in Warren County the head
of a girl killed on prom night is said to bounce on car hoods.

Unspecified "eerie noises" haunt Spook Hollow in Holmes
County on Twp Rd. 329 just outside Holmesville.

Indian Hill's "Spooky Hollow Road" is chilly even on warm
days and gives a horrid impression that people have been hanged
in the area, particularly at the railroad trestle.

Stumpy's Hollow, west of Norwich, is haunted by a headless
figure that used to ride along with travelers.

A house in Killbuck, Holmes Co., was haunted by a ghost
who crept around the house to the sound of rubber sneakers.[37]

A headless freight conductor haunts the Lake Erie & Western
Railroad line between Findlay and Fostoria.[38]

"The Licking River Ghost" rattles windows in homes around
Zanesville's "Y" bridge.[39]

Dead Man's Hollow, near Bucyrus, was haunted by a
murdered man who warned of impending deaths.

A murder or suicide victim is still seen hanging at Hangman's
Hollow, just west of the Ohio 177 and Ohio 130 intersection.[40]

Hiram Perkins, mild-mannered math teacher and pig farmer,
stargazes from beyond the grave at Perkins Observatory on Rt. 23

near Delaware.

New-fallen snow lay in smooth drifts outside the Ostrander farmhouse. Phyllis Powell and her six sisters sat at the kitchen table eating breakfast with their mother.

"For some reason, I looked out the window," recalled Phyllis, "and I saw something come out of the open door of the barn. It looked like a thing in a white, hooded monk's robe, with arms hanging down at its sides. It didn't really have a face, only something glowing that were possibly eyes. It floated rather than walked, gliding about 15 feet from the barn. There was dead silence in the room. Everyone sat with their cereal spoons frozen in mid-air.

"I said, 'Are you seeing what I'm seeing?' Then my mother yelled at my brother, 'Eddie! What are you doing making your brother do all the farm work out there?'

"As she said that, I looked out the window. The white-hooded figure was gone. And my brother's voice came from the bedroom, 'What are you talking about? Marvin is back here.' Eddie and Marvin went out to the barn, but they found no thing, no footprints, nothing."

Jan Materni used to be a tour guide at the Wood County Historical Society Museum. The building served as the Wood County Poor House from the 1900s to 1937. Later it was used as a nursing home. "I always felt like people were watching me; if I looked real quick, somebody would be there," Jan said.

Another volunteer was working in the community room, downstairs in the center wing on the south side. He thought he heard a door slam and went out in the hall to look. There he saw an old lady shuffling down the hall. He nodded and said "hi" to her and turned to go back into the room. "Huh?" he thought, realizing she was in pyjamas, "there's something strange about this lady." He turned back and she was gone.

Part of the building had been the Lunatic House. Said Jan, "I could hear people screaming. There were bars on the windows and steel doors. I could feel people clawing on the doors. I went in there once and that was enough. Once as I was walking by, I looked up and there was a young boy at the window. He was not crazy, but retarded and he was crying because he wanted to go home. He didn't belong there. Is this my imagination or....?

APPENDIX 2
HAUNTING PLACES
Sites open to the public

ASHTABULA CO.

Ashtabula County District Library, 335 W. 44th St., Astabula, OH 44004 (216) 977-9341

CLERMONT CO.

Chateau Laroche, Loveland (513) 683-4686 Tours or directions.

CUYAHOGA CO.

Federal Reserve Bank of Cleveland, East 6th and Superior Ave., Cleveland, OH 44114 (216) 579-2000

Squire's Castle, North Chagrin Reserve

ERIE CO.

Cedar Point Amusement Park, 1 Cedar Point, Sandusky, OH 44870 (419) 626-0830

Merry Go Round Museum, W. Washington and Jackson St., Sandusky, OH (419) 626-6111

FRANKLIN CO.

The Clock Restaurant, 161 N. High St., Columbus, OH 43415 (614) 221-2562

Otterbein College, Cowan Hall, Westerville, OH 43081 (614) 890-0004

Ohio Dominican College, Sansbury Hall, Columbus, OH 43219 (614) 251-4505

GREENE CO.

Sugar Creek Reserve, 7636 Wilmington Pike, Dayton, OH (513) 433-0004 (Maintenance office)

Blue Jacket, 520 S. Stringtown Rd., Xenia, OH 45385 (513) 376-4318 box office.

HAMILTON CO.

Cincinnati Museum of Art, Eden Park Dr., Cincinnati, OH 45202 (513) 721-5204

Westwood Town Hall, Harrison and Montana Avenues in Cincinnati
LUCAS
Chadwick Inn, 301 River Rd., Maumee, OH 43536 (419) 893-2388.
Collingwood Arts Center, 2413 Collingwood Blvd., Toledo, OH 43620-1153 (419) 244-ARTS
Columbian House, 3 N. River Rd., Waterville, OH 43566, (419) 878-3006
MEDINA
Hinckley Library, Intersection of St. Routes 303 and 94, Hinckley, OH
MONTGOMERY CO.
The Old Courthouse, 7 N. Main St., Dayton, OH 45402 (513) 228-6271
Elinor's Amber Rose, 1400 Valley St., Dayton, OH 45404 (513) 228-2511
Frankenstein's Castle, Patterson Ave., Hills & Dales Park
OTTAWA CO.
Johnson Island Cemetery, island accessible from a causeway across Sandusky Bay from Bay Shore Rd.
PERRY CO.
Otterbein Cemetery, Route 22 out of Somerset
PICKAWAY CO.
Village House Restaurant, 72 Long St., Ashville, OH (614) 983-3481
PIKE CO.
Pike Lake Park, between US 50 and SR 124
PREBLE CO.
Ft. St. Clair, follow signs on Rt. 122 or 732 out of Eaton.
TRUMBULL CO.
Warren City Hall, 391 Mahoning NW, Warren, OH
VINTON
Hope Furnace, Route 278 north of Lake Hope
WOOD
Wood County Historical Society Museum, 13660 County Home Rd., Bowling Green, OH 43402 (419) 352-0967

MORE GHOSTLY TALES

(See also the Bibliographies in *Haunted Ohio* and *Haunted Ohio II*)

Let me start off with a plug for my catalog *Invisible Ink: Books on Ghosts & Hauntings®*, the only catalog in the visible world devoted exclusively to books on ghosts. If you're looking for ghost stories—fact or fiction—you'll find over 600 books on ghosts from around the world.

Visit us online at **www.invink.com**.

Fisher, Joe, *Hungry Ghosts: An Investigation into Channeling and the Spirit World*, (1990)

While I found myself irritated at first by Fisher's naive and gullible quest for psychic enlightenment, he redeemed himself in the final chapters where the whole carefully constructed spirit world unravels. Should be required reading for anyone interested in spirit communication.

Hauck, Dennis William, *The National Directory of Haunted Places, A guidebook to ghostly abodes, sacred sites, UFO landings, and other supernatural locations*, (1994)

A truly encyclopedic reference. Stories from every state. Nicely arranged for ease of use, directions to most sites, and lots and lots of photos. List of Organizations, References

Hufford, David J., *The Terror that comes in the night: An Experience-Centered Study of Supernatural Assault Traditions*

Have you ever been "hag-ridden" or wakened to find a body pressing down with suffocating force on your chest? Discusses various possible causes for "the Hag" including the intriguing theory that incubi and succubi are a form of sleep apnea!

Myers, Arthur, *The Ghosthunter's Guide: To Haunted Parks, Churches, Historical Landmarks & Other Public Places*, (1992)

If you like to visit haunt-spots, here's a guide to some places open to the public.

Peach, Emily, *Things That Go Bump in the Night, How to Investigate and Challenge Ghostly Experiences,* (1991)

A practical, down-to-earth set of guidelines for recognizing, understanding, and coping with paranormal phenomena. Detailed info on how to approach an investigation—how to evaluate the witnesses' experiences, what questions to ask, what points to look out for and how to examine the evidence in a clear and straightforward way. An exceptionally sensible book!

Swetnam, George, *Devils, Ghosts, and Witches: Occult Folklore of the Upper Ohio Valley*, (1988)

Witches and warlocks and Indian ghosts, oh my! Ghostly and occult folklore from Pennsylvania, West Virginia, Ohio, and Kentucky.

Underwood, Peter, *Ghosts and How to See Them,* (1993)

Underwood, President and Chief Investigator of Britain's Ghost Club,tells how to conduct an investigation, how to photograph psychic phenomena, and where and when ghosts are most likely to be seen—a question I am frequently asked. I had to leaf through this very carefully so I didn't get a nasty shock from some of the wonderful photographs! A calendar of haunt-spots around the world and a list of useful organizations is included. This is an excellent guide for beginner or expert.

USA Weekend Editors, *I Never Believed in Ghosts Until...100 Real-Life Encounters,* (1992)

These very personal stories submitted to USA Weekend offer a fascinating variety of ghosts.

Wilson, Colin, *Poltergeist: A Study in Destructive Haunting,* (1993)

Wilson covers poltergeist "symptoms", possession, elementals, fairies, ley lines and earth energy, witchcraft, ghosts and psychoanalysis. I've always accepted Dr. Nandor Fodor's theories that poltergeists arise from a troubled individual's unconscious, but this book is making me think again.

REFERENCES

Prelude - The Flames

[1]*Lima News,* 31 Oct. 1984 B1

Chapter One - Home is Where the Haunt Is

[1] Martha Foster, "Grandpappy" *Ohio Magazine,* (Dec. 1988)

Chapter Two - The Ghost in the Machine

[1]"Strange sounds, images reported from barn," *The Alliance Review,*
    10 Mar. 1983

Chapter Three - Stairway to Heaven

[1] "The Strange Death of Frederick Zimmerman," *Ohio Valley Folktale
    Research Project,* (Chillicothe, OH: The Ross County Historical Society)

Chapter Four - Lanterns for the Dead

[1] "The Legend of Mary," *Haunting Tales of Fairfield County,* (Lancaster,
    Fairfield County District Library, 1980)

Chapter Five - Caution! Ghosts at Work

[1] Bill Sammon, "Fed bank refuses to give currency to haunting tale," *Plain
    Dealer,* 14 Aug. 1992, 1A, 10A

[2] Russell Frey, *Rogue's Hollow* (n.p. 1958), 94, 96-7

[3] Gloria Brown, "Haunting Hinckley," *Library Live!* [Medina Co. Public
    Library] Vol. 5, No. 3 (Summer 1992)

Chapter Six - The Haunted Trunk

[1] Marguerite Blair, "Mirror, Mirror," *Ohio Valley Folktale Research Project,*
    (Chillicothe, OH, The Ross County Historical Society, 1957)

[2] "The Butler County Courthouse Ghost", article by Jim Blount

[3] Lisa Fatzinger, "Ghostly Goings On," *The Advertiser-Tribune,* 27 Oct. 1991

Chapter Seven - Men in Black

[1] Tim Gaffney, "Ghost Stories from the Miami Valley," *Dayton Daily News,* 28
    Oct. 1984

[2] E. Moesta Sharp, *Who is That in the Mirror?* (The Author) 105-108

[3] "Jeffrey C. Hawkins," "A Haunting in Hyde Park," *Cincinnati Enquirer,* 31
    Oct. 1990 1C, 7C

Chapter Eight - The Spirit of the Waters

[1] *Eaton Register,* 24 Dec. 1868; Lloyd and Marilyn Petry, *The Birth of Fort St.
    Clair 1792-1992,* (The Authors, 1992) 12

[2] *Delaware Gazette,* 31 Oct. 1992, quoting *Delaware Gazette,* 18 Sept. 1868

"The Strange, Sad Spirit of the Scioto," Jean Anderson, *The Haunting of
    America: Ghost Stories from Our Past,* (Boston: Houghton-Mifflin Co.,
    1973) 113-121; Rae D. Henkle, "A Native Ghost," *The Ohio Magazine,*
    (Vol. 4, 1908) 55-59

[3] Darlene Prince, "Seen any ghosts? Your neighbors have." *The Crescent-
    News,* 31 Oct. 1993

[4] "Ghouling down the river," *Cincinnati Post,* 17 May 1977 14

[5] Russell Ramsey, Jr., "The Choir master's mystery," *Sandusky Register,* 25
    Oct. 1987

Chapter Nine - The Show Must Go On—and On

[1] *Cincinnati Commercial,* 22 Oct. 1876 8; Mike Turmell, "Human bones found under Music Hall," *Cincinnati Enquirer,* 7 May 1988 1A, 8A; *Cincinnati Post,* 7 May 1988 1A; *Cincinnati Post,* 20 May 1988 1

[2] Michael Grossberg, *Columbus Dispatch,* 4 Feb. 1990 quoted in *On Campus* vol. 5 no. 11 (March 12, 1990) and Gregory Davis, "Twyla and Friends," *Tan & Cardinal* [Otterbein college paper] 25 Oct. 1990

Chapter Eleven - Highways to Hell

[1] *The Haunted Stump or The Story of the Amputated Hands,* Erasmus Foster Darby, [pseud. David Knowlton Webb] (Chillicothe, OH: The Author, 1953)

[2] Lonnie E. Legge, "I never heard the train that killed me," *FATE,* Vol. 12, (Oct. 1959) 79-81

[3] "Aluminum Paint Hides Bridge's Gory History," *Lima News,* 27 Feb. 1949

Chapter Twelve - A Ghost's Home is His Castle

[1] Julian Cavalier, *American Castles* (NY: A.S. Barnes and Company, 1973) 169-233-5 and personal letter from Carl Cassavecchia, Cleveland Metroparks

[2] Cavalier, *op. cit.* 169-174; *Cincinnati Enquirer,* 18 Nov. 1979; *Miami Valley Sunday Magazine,* 18 Jan. 1981

[3] *Columbus Dispatch,* 22 May 1993

[4] *Cleveland Press,* 27 Mar. 1980; *Ohio Magazine,* Nov. 1980; *Plain Dealer,* 11 May 1975; Barbara Dreimiller, "A Dream of Things That Were," *Western Reserve Magazine,* July-August 1976; *Plain Dealer News & Home Listings Guide,* 8 Dec./14 Dec. 1989; *Cleveland Plain Dealer Sunday Magazine,* 23 Oct. 1973; *Cleveland Plain Dealer* "PD Action," 28 Feb. 1975

Chapter Thirteen - Tales from the Crypt

[1] *Elyria Chronicle-Telegram/Sunday Scene,* 30 Oct. 1977

[2] *Piqua Daily Call,* 15 Sept. 1973, 20 Sept. 1973

[3] "The Legend of the Horseshoe Gravestone," *Somerset Press,* 19 Apr. 1973

[4] "Seen By Thousands; Never Identified; 'Eugene' Buried With Dignity," *Sabina News Record,* 22 Oct. 1964

[5] *Dayton Daily News,* 5 June 1993 4D

[6] *The Paulding Progress,* 26 Oct. 1983

[7] *The Post,* 31 Oct. 1978

[8] Robert Hull, *Mad Marshall County: The Grit and Spirit of Mid-Ohioans* (Bay Village, OH: Bob Hull Books & Features, 1981) 261-3

Chapter Fourteen - High Spirits

[1] *Toledo Blade,* 21 June 1935; *Toledo Blade,* 28 June 1948

[2] Dale Huffman, "Nothing scary going on, just a ghost in the attic," *Dayton Daily News,* 31 Oct. 1992

[3] *Columbus Dispatch,* 18 Oct. 1988 1C

Chapter Fifteen - The Thrill of Fear

[1] Virginia Santore, "The Vengeful Succubus," *FATE,* (September, 1977) 43-46

[2] The Rev. Gerald Hunter, "Where the Past is Present," *Akron Beacon Journal, Magazine,* 25 Oct. 1992 6

[3] Virginia Santore, "The House That Hated People," *FATE,* (October 1963) 80-85

[4] *Collingwood Arts Center Newsletter,* Vol. 5, No. 4 (Oct./Nov. 1992)
Research by Eric Beach and Jim Beard

Appendix One - Fright Bites

[1] Sam Roe, "Does murder victim haunt Trilby house?" *Toledo Blade,* no date

[2] Charles Grim, *The Ohio and Michigan War and Tales of the Border,* (The Author, 1960) 17-18

[3] James E. Leasure, "The Headless Horseman of Cherry Hill" (Chillicothe, OH: Dave Webb, 1953)

[4] Mary Jo Cloran, "The Demon," *Ohio Legends,* Members of the Ohio Federation of Women's Clubs, (Canton, 1984) 299

[5] Harold Igo, "The Headless Soldier," *Yellow Springs News,* 8 Apr. 1943

[6] Mitch Weiss, "Towns die, legends don't," *Fremont News-Messenger,* 18 Oct. 1988

[7] Curtis Otwell, private letter, 1972, Darke Co. Hist. Soc.

[8] Petry, *op. cit.* 12

[9] *ibid*

[10] Walter F. Williams, *Haunted Depot?* (Galion: The Author, 1991)

[11] Clyde Dorn, "The Miamiville trainman's ghost," *Cincinnati Enquirer,* 13 July 1980 6-9

[12] Joel Rudinger, *Folklore of Erie County, Ohio,* (Bowling Green State University: Ph.D. dissertation, 1971) 103-4

[13] Paula Miner, "Ghosts Still Haunt Area Graveyards," *Toledo Blade,* 31 Oct. 1978

[14] *ibid*

[15] Connie Cartmell, "'George' roams sorority," *Marietta Times,* 30-31 Oct. 1993 1D

[16] "Ghosts that Roam Ohio State Park Lands, *Toledo Blade,* 31 Oct. 1982

[17] Richard C. Widman, "To grab the brass ring," *Plain Dealer,* 18 Apr. 1986; letter from Shelly Luipold, Merry Go Round Museum

[18] Connie Rohr, "Ashville restaurant home to mischievous spirit," *Circleville Herald,* 27 Oct. 1993

[19] Velma Griffin, "Is it really haunted?' *Carroll Times Reporter,* no date

[20] *The Post,* 31 Oct. 1978

[21] "The Phantom House of Crown City," *FATE,* (June 1953) 8-9

[22] Lois Zizert, "A Ghost Story that is True," (Lewisburg, OH, The Author)

[23] John A. Rayner, The First Century of Piqua Ohio, (Piqua, OH: *The Magee Bros Publishing Co.,* 1916) 203-4 and Martha Hardcastle, "Ghost Stories: Piqua has its share," *Piqua Daily Call,* 31 Oct. 1991 1

[24] *The Lima News,* 13 Nov. 1992 1 A6

[25] John Switzer, "Fort Hayes Ghosts Await Halloween Tours," *Columbus Dispatch,* 26 Oct. 1991

[26] Julia Keller, "The Haunting of Ohio Dominican," *Columbus Dispatch*, 19 Jan. 1988 1E

[27] *Cincinnati Enquirer*, 31 Oct. 1993

[28] *Cincinnati Enquirer*, 31 Oct. 1982 7-12

[29] *Cincinnati Enquirer*, 12 Apr. 1981 9-17

[30] Joe B. McKnight, "Wooooo Waynesville! Does the past haunt it?" *Dayton Daily News*, 30 Oct. 1983; Mary Sikora, "The Haunting of Waynesville," *Dayton Daily News*, 4 Aug. 1978

[31] Connie Cartmell, "Stories of Ghost Linger at Mansion," *Dayton Daily News*, 18 Oct. 1992 9B

[32] Marilyn Petry, private letter, 1993

[33] *ibid*

[34] *Toledo Blade,* 3 Aug. 1972 1, 4; *Columbus Dispatch,* 9 Aug. 1972; *Toledo Blade*, 10 Aug. 1972 34

[35] *Philadelphia Press*, 25 Mar., 1894 and Adi-Kent Thomas Jeffrey, "The Murder Victim Refused to Stay Dead," *Cincinnati Enquirer*, 26 Oct. 1968 23

[36] Jim Blount, private letter, 1994

[37] *Democratic Standard of Coshocton,* 1 Feb. 1889

[38] *Erie County Reporter*, 23 Jan. 1890

[39] *Zanesville Times Signal,* 9 Apr. 1912

[40] "The Legend of Hangman's Hollow," article by Jim Blount

INDEX

GENERAL INDEX

INDEX OF STORIES BY LOCATION

NOTE! *PLEASE DO NOT TEAR OUT THIS PAGE. XEROX THIS FORM OR COPY YOUR ORDER ONTO A SHEET OF PAPER.*

HOW TO ORDER
YOUR OWN AUTOGRAPHED COPIES OF
THE *HAUNTED OHIO* SERIES
Visit our web site at www.invink.com

Call **(937) 426-5110** with your VISA or MasterCard order or send this order form to: **Kestrel Publications, 1811 Stonewood Dr., Beavercreek, OH 45432 • Fax (937) 320-1832**

_____ copies of *GHOST HUNTER'S GUIDE* @ $16.95 ea.	$_____
_____ copies of *HAUNTED OHIO* @ $12.95 each	$_____
_____ copies of *HAUNTED OHIO II* @ $12.95 each	$_____
_____ copies of *HAUNTED OHIO III* @ $12.95 each	$_____
_____ copies of *HAUNTED OHIO IV* @ $12.95 each	$_____
_____ copies of *HAUNTED OHIO V* @ $15.95 HB each	$_____
_____ copies of *SPOOKY OHIO* @ $9.95 each	$_____

+ $3.50 Media Mail s/h for the first
item, $1.50 for each additional item.   **Sales Tax** $_____
Write invisiblei@aol.com or call   **S/H** $_____
(937) 426-5110 for speedier mail options.   **TOTAL** $_____
Ohio shipping addresses add 7% sales tax.

NOTE: We usually ship the same or next day. Please allow three weeks before you panic. If a book *has* to be somewhere by a certain date, let us know so we can try to get it there on time.

MAIL TO (Please print clearly and include your phone number)

_____
_____
_____
_____

FREE AUTOGRAPH!

If you would like your copies autographed, please print the name or names to be inscribed. _____

_____

PAYMENT MADE BY:

☐ Check   ☐ MasterCard   ☐ VISA
($15 min. order on credit cards)

Card No. _____   Expiration Date:

Signature _____   Mo_____ Yr_____